The Path to Leadership

DISCOVER YOUR INNER STRENGTH

Kalyani Patnaik

JAICO PUBLISHING HOUSE

Ahmedabad Bangalore Bhopal Chennai
Delhi Hyderabad Kolkata Lucknow Mumbai

Published by Jaico Publishing House
A-2 Jash Chambers, 7-A Sir Phirozshah Mehta Road
Fort, Mumbai - 400 001
jaicopub@jaicobooks.com
www.jaicobooks.com

THE PATH TO LEADERSHIP
ISBN 978-93-90166-69-5

First Jaico Impression: 2021

Page design and layout: Jojy Philip, Delhi

*This book is dedicated to my beloved brother,
late Surgeon Captain Prabhakar Patro—a true leader
mentoring medical students, who left for his heavenly
abode in October 2020 as a Covid warrior.*

CONTENTS

NOTE FROM THE AUTHOR

The leader is one who forges ahead of others by walking the path first. *The Path to Leadership* is my maiden venture. I have thought about the subject over the years during my experience with students at school and interactions with people I met in everyday life. So the works are based on examples and inspiring anecdotes gathered over the years.

Everybody aspires to be a leader and enjoy the empowerment but there is no fixed formula to become one. Not all managers are good leaders nor do all academicians become successful leaders. All individuals have the skills lying dormant within them, but to identify these skills is an art. This book provides a direction and creates a structure to support it by realising the innate potential and harnessing the talent to help one become a leader. The ingredients for success provide the information one needs to improve one's leadership skills.

Information is power. To combat any war successfully, a leader needs to be well-informed. Teachers can help students make better decisions by using powerful insights and gathering correct information. Data collection, its analysis and interpretation help the leader make the best decision.

This journey of leadership is a personal reflection after spending several years in academics. It is therefore the outcome of my thoughts on leadership through the course of my work experience. The letter 'I' has been specially chosen because a leader is the only identity at any given point of a situation.

To help readers realise their potential, self-assessment tools have been provided. I hope that this book will help ignite your mind and you will continue to improve long after reading it.

1

THE 'I' OF LEADERSHIP

"Who am I?" Has this question ever haunted you? It's a deep conversation starter, one that not only puts you on a journey of self-discovery, but also unpacks the infinite potential that exists within you, untapped, ready to be explored. You simply cannot ignore the 'I' within you, which urges you to be your best, to blossom into the person you dream of becoming, the leader that you are. Wherever you go, whatever you do, whomsoever you follow, the 'I' rears its head, reminding you that all you need exists within you.

Look around. Birds, animals and other creatures are constantly imparting valuable lessons on how to maximise our true potential. Each one does its bit, whether it's an ant or an eagle, a bee or an elephant, contributing to their communities, being leaders in their own right. We are a part of the same ecosystem. We couldn't be too different.

Aristotle, one of the greatest Greek philosophers, stated, "Man is by nature a social animal; an individual who is unsocial naturally and not accidently is either beneath our notice or more than social."

Whenever I read this quote I wonder, did mankind learn from the animal kingdom how to exist in society, or has the animal kingdom learnt from mankind to live in herds and packs? The answers I repeatedly stumble upon are that our planet earth existed long before mankind, and so did nature. Mankind has improvised what the animal kingdom has shown them through the ages. I am convinced that this is a fact; mankind follows the animal kingdom closely to work towards supremacy.

Another question that comes to my mind is—did the leader of the pack create the herd, or did the herd create the leader of the pack? This question seems to have no answers. It's quite like asking what came first: the chicken or the egg. No one has been able to verify this. We do know that chickens are needed to lay eggs, and the eggs hatch into chicks that grow into chickens.

Nature and the animal kingdom have influenced me greatly. I am in awe of the majesty of the animal kingdom. Ever watched a documentary about animals and their habitats? It amazes me how naturally hierarchy is respected. The leader of every pack or herd commands respect, without having to raise a flag or wage a war.

The leader is graceful, gentle, regal, majestic, disciplined, watchful, caring, responsible, strong, courageous, empathetic, protective, assertive and loyal. These are the innate characteristics of the ideal leaders of mankind. The world has seen several such leaders, whose sterling qualities have inspired mankind all through the ages.

Leadership is not about aggression, stubbornness, despondency or dictatorship. On the contrary, it is about leading the team as a unit, and not walking ahead alone expecting others to follow. It's about inspiring the team to walk along, and contribute to the collective progress of fellow team members. Leadership is not about dictating rules and expecting everyone to follow them blindly. It's about leading by example, walking the talk, leading from the front, co-establishing the rules of the game, and establishing a common platform together.

Have you ever noticed a flock of birds flying in the sky in a V-formation? It is a beautiful sight to watch one bird lead the others in a formation that helps them save energy while flying long distances and keeps them safe while migrating. The leader at the centre manoeuvres the entire flock to safety. There are no ego tussles here. In fact, I am sure the leader does not even tell the rest, "I am your leader, follow me." It just happens naturally, as the strongest in the flock wins the confidence of the rest. It's an act based on trust. The flock knows that their leader will take them to the migratory zone safely and within the required time span.

If you think of evolution, being an animal precedes being human. Being in nature precedes being in our built-up cities.

Like birds in flight, we can learn an invaluable leadership lesson from a pack of wolves. They walk in a straight line with the one at the front creating a trail for those following behind. The formation is such that the first couple of wolves are normally the old or sick; the next set is the strongest that protects the pack from the front. Following them are the wolves with their pups that are protected by another set of strong members walking behind them. At the end is the leader of the pack, who ensures that no one is left behind. He keeps the pack tight on the same path. He is ready to sprint in any direction to protect the entire pack. Effective leadership is not always about leading from the front; leading from the back can be as effective.

It's all about being one with the team, amalgamating or merging oneself with it.

We often speak of herd mentality—people following someone blindly. We believe that everybody prefers to follow the whims and fancies of others, quite like the baby lion cub, growing up among a flock of sheep. He eats grass and behaves like the sheep he follows, till he realises his actual identity when he encounters a lion. This happens to people across all ages. They follow others simply to "fit in and not be left out". Textbooks call this peer pressure; I consider it herd mentality.

You could argue that if we can admire a flock of geese following a leader in a V-formation, or the leader wolf leading the pack from behind, then why not simply follow a leader, or be led by one? Well, I believe that you must recognise your individuality and the uniqueness that you can contribute to the group. Don't be a mindless follower. Be a leading team player. You can be a leader of your own life. After all, every goose in the flock takes its own position, based on its power and abilities. Each one ahead of the other makes it easier for the rest while flying. This ensures that no matter how weak a goose is, or how strong, the weak lead the strong, migrating together, soaring the skies.

Sheep are an important part of the ecosystem. They contribute to the well-being of nature and the human population. They are unique creatures, and they have their own hierarchy with a leader of the herd. The lion is higher up in the hierarchy of the animal kingdom. So, being mindless of its own majesty, power, strength and position, and following the sheep blindly, is foolishness.

This has been beautifully summed up by Swami Vivekananda, a spiritual leader who at a young age, took spirituality to the western world: "Come up, O lions, and shake off the delusion that you are sheep; you are souls immortal, spirits free, blest and eternal; ye are not matter, ye are not bodies; matter is your servant, not you the servant of matter." Though his life was cut short because of cancer, his legacy continues to live on.

Leadership is not a new word or concept. It was coined and created the day mankind came to recognise the need for co-existence. Human beings needed to live together as a group to protect themselves from every adversity. They also needed a leader to help manoeuvre them through storms to safety. The leaders created small groups to form communities. Communities grew into societies.

Societies expanded into villages that grew into towns that developed into cities forming states and creating nations. As mankind expanded, the approach and perception of leadership kept changing.

Most understand leadership to be another word for authority and power. This holds true for the lexicon experts, and otherwise. However, my experience has taught me that grooming every student to be a leader shapes them into the finest citizens. They are decisive, strong, courageous, confident, compassionate, ready to serve, humble, empathetic, gentle, assertive and self-aware and prepared to take risks in their careers. These are traits that define effective and efficient leadership. One can lead others effectively only when one can first lead oneself to hold positions of responsibility at every tier.

The individuality of every being is its power and it is possible to harness this inherent potential. When you say, "I dream I can, and I must attain my goal," the primary factor is 'I'. The whole power of desiring, dreaming and then working towards its attainment or fulfilment lies within the entity itself.

If there is no will and drive, then pushing yourself forward is only a futile exercise, like a gas balloon that will burst or deflate in due course of time. Effective leaders, whose work amplifies under the force of will, actually make things happen for society.

Sheryl Sandberg, COO of Facebook, sums it up well when she says, "Leadership, after all, is about making others better as a result of your presence and making sure that the impact lasts in your absence." Well, according to research, elephants are proof that a leader has to be a team player first.

Whenever, I think about effective leadership, the queen bee, who presides over her populous hive, mesmerises me with her leadership skills. Do you know hives consist of approximately over 60,000 bees? The queen bee buzzes away busily along with the rest of the bees while constructing the beehive for honey; and yet every bee is worked to its strengths to maximise the honey production. Leadership and team working at their best!

Effective and efficient communication skills are an extremely important quality of successful leaders. We can learn the art of communicating effectively from dolphins. Communication is not only about what is said, but also what is heard—verbally and/or non-verbally expressed. From tail slapping to vocal calls, dolphins use several methods of communication to lead, direct and protect each other.

I have great respect for the quote from the book *Animal Farm* by George Orwell: "All animals are equal, but some animals are more equal than others." The more equal ones are leaders that lead the less equal ones.

Sapiens have not only learnt a great deal on leadership from fauna, but also flora.

We may consider ourselves to be the most intelligent species on earth, but we tend to endanger ourselves by falling out of focus because of the wired network in our brain. Animals and plants are wired to focus on their goal only. The human brain is fantastically wired to think numerous thoughts and imbibe as many at a go to lead.

We tend to describe someone 'as elegant as an elm tree' or suggest that one should be 'as majestic as an oak tree'. These metaphors can be used for humans as well. Leaders, no doubt, are elegant and majestic, amongst other qualities.

A couple of years ago when I visited the Muir woods in San Francisco, I was awestruck by the huge redwood trees that spoke not only of firm roots and soaring ambitions, but also reminded me that I am a leader, and can create leaders. This I learnt observing the burls growing on them. Healthy burls are reproduction strategies of these trees. A redwood tree is a sturdy stalwart and superlatively statuesque. At that moment, my heart told me, "I choose to be a leader like these redwood trees."

We learn from plants and trees to be firmly rooted. If our ideas and qualities get uprooted, it is because of the weak foundation of ideas held by leaders themselves. No strong, full-grown tree falls due to the wind and gale; it bends moderately as the breeze blows during storms powerfully, in order to brave the severe storm. Trees grow tall, spanning the sky with their vision. The most beautiful of trees bear fruits and drop seeds for more trees to grow, leading to a flourishing forest. If we allow our vision to be a tad lofty, we can see that success is the fruit one bears and the legacy one leaves behind, just like trees.

American artist Georgia Totto O'Keeffe inspiringly said, "When you take a flower in your hand and really look at it, it's your world for the moment." How beautiful it is to reflect upon the fact that nature has great lessons for us. We humans blossom in love and sunshine. Like a lotus, we become strong in spite of the dirt and the filthy water around us.

Great leaders emerge stronger through harsh weather, and blizzards and storms, and through every obstacle and challenge, manoeuvring their teams to write success stories, inspiring new leaders to bloom and blossom.

One day, I was sitting in the lap of nature when a question popped up in my mind: "Do you know what makes concrete jungle world leaders different from the leaders of the natural kingdom?" This question fascinated me and I decided to explore it further.

I took my special pen and my little majestic notebook (they are my faithful companions that help me to build a reservoir of experience and inspiration gained from my observations), opened it to an empty page, started doodling animals and labelling their unique leadership traits. On the opposite page, I doodled a human stick figure and listed the leadership traits unique to humankind.

What I noticed was that while each animal-leader has one particular trait, an ideal human-leader has multiple traits imbibed from the unique traits of each creature of nature. What's incredible is that they are constantly being polished and ever-changing. The only thing that is constant, after all, is change. The core ideal responsibility of every animal leader is leading their pack to safety. On the other hand, every human-leader has multiple roles to play to lead others to being leaders themselves.

The human leader has an identity, which stems from the 'I'ness of being. This simply means that every attribute of leadership is all about polishing every 'I' of one's 'Identity'.

This concept gave me a whole new understanding of not only what makes a leader great, but also what goes to make brilliant leaders. A new perspective of leadership dawned. I realised that everybody is born to lead their lives, and they keep getting better with every 'Improvement' of every 'I'.

This begins by recognising that when we say we are 'leading' our lives, it's not about merely existing or going through the motions; it's about assuming the title role, about being a conscious protagonist, about 'leading' one's life by conscious design, purposefully, and with eyes wide open. When you lead your life responsibly, you are empowered to empower others. Great leaders are not those who have the greatest number of followers, but those who inspire great numbers to lead their lives to realise their highest potential.

The journey to effective leadership begins with the self, extending to 'Inspire' many.

You are your primary responsibility. You are your own leader. You are your own leadership legend.

It takes the 'Integration' of every 'I' of your identity to be an ideal leader. Developing each 'I' to make you the complete, ideal leader is a constant, continuous process. It is not one more or less important than the other, nor is it about more of some 'I's and less of other 'I's. It is truly about the effective use of each 'I', according to the situation ahead of you.

What I have learnt through every experience is that I lead my life through challenges; which may be as personal as my health, or as professional as being the Principal of a school, by picking up the 'I's of my identity and using them as per the requirement.

For instance, when I have to lead myself back to good health, I use the following 'I's—Inspiration to recover faster, Integrity to choose to eat healthy and not cheat, Insightfulness to understand what caused my body to break down, Intuitiveness to understand what my body truly needs—and voila, in no time, I am healthy again.

Let me give you an example of a professional situation where I was needed to lead my students to confident participation in an inter-school competition. Here, I used, first and foremost, Innovativeness; it provided me with the ability to Inspire students to utilise their unique individual strengths. Next, I had to be Industrious to constantly and patiently guide them to put in efforts to polish their skills. Integrity was a powerful tool to ensure they used fair play in the field. Insightfulness helped them become aware of the opponents' strategies and counter them mindfully. Imagination was important to be solution-oriented when faced with a problem. The team set off confidently, enjoyed the game, and at most times, returned with a bagful of experiences, even though they were not always victorious.

Experience and learning is a bigger reward than all the biggest awards!

To be an effective leader, you need to first understand and develop every 'I' of leadership by banishing the 'I' of ego, by leading your life by example, with total discipline and dedication, extremely effectively and efficiently.

2

IMAGINATION

"Imagination is like a muscle. I found out that the more I wrote, the bigger it got."

— Philip Jose Farmer

While etymologically the word 'imagination' has strong roots in Latin, as a skill, it has been studied and put to tremendous use in the 21st century. This is not to say that imagination was not used by human beings through history. That is not possible, as imagination is an important and vital faculty of the mind. However, while it was a word used in language, it was not considered a skill or a concept that needed to be studied and understood. It was simply a taken-for-granted faculty, probably hidden backstage, as creativity has always been regarded as intrinsic to every venture, through the ages.

Imagination is more like the scriptwriter, who brings creativity to the forefront. Images in the mind precede their manifestation into reality.

Albert Einstein once stated, "Imagination is more important than knowledge." This definitely holds true for all science fiction. It has all been figments of the authors' imagination. For example, Jules Verne, one of the first, and amongst the greatest leaders of science fiction writers, who could fathom the depth of the sea and the possible journey to the centre of the earth. Long before the invention of navigable aircrafts and submarines, Verne had already described space, air and underwater travel in his writings.

Right from his childhood, Indian mathematician Srinivasa Ramanujan spent time imagining and digging deep into numbers. He did not have formal training in pure mathematics, but that did not deter him. His contributions to number theory, continued fractions, infinite series and mathematical analysis have ranked him among the foremost minds in mathematics.

Acharya JC Bose was a polymath, physicist, biologist, botanist, archaeologist and a leader in his own areas of specialisation. He spoke to plants and played music to them, imagining that they were responding. This became practicable when the Crescograph was invented, proving that plants do have feelings and are responsive; hence imagination turned into reality.

There is no doubt that the power of the imagination made Bill Gates and Steve Jobs take personal computers to the humungous heights they have achieved. They are considered amongst the leading drivers of change in information technology and in the way we experience our world.

Who are these leaders? Are they inventors or discoverers? They are thought leaders who imagine and manifest their imagination into reality. Imagination leads to discoveries, and ultimately to inventions. Hence, we can presume that leaders imagine first and then invent.

To be an effective leader, you need to allow free flow of the mind's ability and skill to imagine.

Just as meditation requires you to sit silently with your eyes closed and focus on a word or a symbol, similarly, the path for every leader is set by what I call the 'leadership symbol'. Just as we are moved by feelings, emotions and images, we are moved by the symbols of leadership.

Michelangelo made a mention of his 'leadership symbol': "I saw the angel in the marble, and carved until I set him free."

The 'leadership symbol' could be in the form of one's ambitions, just as in the case of Jamshedji Tata, whose symbol was "business", within which he imagined Hospitality, Industry and Research. He developed all three wings of his business symbol, which has etched him in history as one of the greatest business leaders ever.

I was cleaning my window sill one early summer morning, when I chanced upon a bird's nest up in the corner. At first, I thought it was a flimsy little thing and could be removed, but the nest was strong and intricately woven, and held a few eggs which the crow must have just laid. That moment was like a boomerang of childhood imaginations and inventions. At that moment of pounding thoughts, I understood the intricacy and ingenuity with which the nest was built. That's when I sighed to myself— here was architecture and innovation at its best, with no formal training; just being one with nature.

Martin Luther King's leadership symbol can be considered as 'equality' that demolishes racism. This young, great leader's speech, which he delivered on 28 August 1963, is said to have ended racism in the USA, as he fought for civil and economic rights.

"I have a dream that my little children will one day live in a nation where they will not be judged by the colour of their skin, but by the content of their character," he famously said.

The Civil Rights Act was passed in 1964 by the US Congress, prohibiting discrimination amongst races. It was Martin Luther King's dream come true.

All imaginative leaders are creative. A leader must brim with ideas in order to be forward-looking. The brain is wired like a labyrinth. To envision what triggers this imagination could be anything as simple as an apple falling on Newton's head, leading to the theory of gravitational force. Or, for that matter, floating in the bathtub can lead you to the 'Eureka!' moment experienced by Archimedes of Syracuse—a great Greek leader of mathematics, physics, engineering and astronomy. He is widely remembered for the Archimedes Principle.

Shakespeare himself emphasises the necessity of dreaming for the creation of art. He suggests, while commenting on his play 'A Midsummer Night's Dream', that imagining alternate realities such as the woods can yield a work of art. Indeed, Shakespeare creates his play from his own imaginings, reflections and dreams.

Once, a drawing teacher asked the class to draw a design of a refrigerator. All but one drew the normal rectangular shaped refrigerator. Only one boy drew an oval refrigerator. The teacher asked him where he had seen such a refrigerator. He simply said, "If the inventors have designed a rectangular refrigerator, then I, with the help of my imagination, can invent an oval refrigerator."

This young boy, a leader in the making, has strong leadership skills and used his imagination to perceive potential possibilities. If pilotless aircrafts exist and driverless cars are becoming a reality, then an oval-shaped refrigerator may not be a distant dream.

What exactly do leaders do when they imagine? All they do is think, sense, reflect on their ideas, build on the images of the mind, research, work on the possibilities, develop, maybe even hit roadblocks, but persevere till they stamp their leadership symbol and leave a mark for others to be inspired.

Interestingly, while we consider imagination to be a faculty of the mind, Dr Murray Hunter of the University of Malaysia Perlis offers eight types of imaginations that individuals are capable of using daily:

- Effectual Imagination, which, according to Dr Hunter, blends all information together in order to create new concepts and ideas.
- Intellectual or Conceptual Imagination is used when one attempts to develop a hypothesis based on fragments one gathers.
- Fantasy Imagination helps one create and develop works of fiction across varied genres and mediums.
- Empathy Imagination, according to Dr Hunter, aids in understanding what one experiences emotionally, from one's own perspective and circumstances.
- Strategic Imagination is all about the vision of possibility—'what could be'.
- Emotional Imagination is connected to the manifestation of emotional dispositions in order to extend them to emotional situations.
- Dreams are considered images created by the subconscious that are brought to the surface when one is asleep.
- Memory Reconstruction is involved when one attempts to retrieve recollections of people, situations or objects.

According to Dr Hunter, "Imagination enables us to create new meanings from cognitive cues or stimuli within the environment, which on occasion can lead to new insights."

A leader should use every type of imagination effectively, creatively, empathetically to create a lasting impression to inspire other leaders to follow suit.

The little tale, 'The Boy and the Cocoon', inspires me to understand the importance of imagination that allows you to be patient while observing nature, rather than impatient, and destroy the probability of a beautiful story unfolding.

A young boy loved butterflies for their wonderful combination of colours. In fact, he used to spend a lot of time around the beautiful fluttering insects. He was aware of how every butterfly struggled to transform from an ugly caterpillar into a majestic creature. However, he had never witnessed it happen.

One day he chanced upon a cocoon. It had a tiny opening. This meant that the butterfly was trying to make its way out. He sat there, for over ten hours, watching the butterfly struggle to break free from its cocoon.

Finally, he felt the butterfly needed help, and so he took out a pair of scissors from his bag, made a larger opening in the cocoon, and pulled out the butterfly.

However, this was not a beautiful large butterfly, but a tiny one with a swollen body and withered wings.

He waited for it to fly. Unfortunately, neither did the wings expand, nor did the swelling subside.

It would not be able to fly, and so it went on to live its life crawling with withered wings.

One of the primary requirements to be an effective leader is patience that nurtures and respects every figment, or as I call it, 'fragment' of the imagination.

Imagination is one of the most precious faculties we are gifted with. If we pay attention to the images created in our mind, then with perseverance and creativity, we become effective leaders. Leadership is not just about leading a large group or big enterprise or a state or a nation. Leadership is about creating a lasting impact on others that inspires them to become a better version of themselves with each passing day, as they observe you doing the same.

For me, the difference between the images of the mind and the images projected by our imagination upon the mind is that the former are paintings of our problems and the latter are pictures of probable solutions.

Every leader from every walk of life, no matter how big the enterprise, invention, discovery or nation, has provided solutions that have brought changes to many a life. Those who have remained with the dark images of magnified problems have remained there, either as followers, or non-achievers.

Take, for instance, the boy in the story of 'The Boy and the Cocoon'. The image transmitted in his mind was that of the problem, and he questioned the process of the struggling butterfly. This made him restless and so, in spite of waiting for 10 hours, he gave in and destroyed the butterfly's future. He created a larger problem.

However, if he had chosen to watch in awe the emergence of the butterfly, allowing it to find its way out of the cocoon, he would have witnessed the unfurling of magic. His imagination would have allowed him to wait on, by reflecting on his mind the actual power of struggle. All great enterprises have gone through immense struggle to bring to the world their solutions.

If you read the biography of every leader, across various walks of life, you will see the common play of struggle on their way to greet success. However, the power of their imagination never allowed them to surrender to the dark pictures of the problems they faced. Their imagination was the primary ingredient in their recipe of success.

It is, therefore, important to empower your imagination to lead your life to the heights of leadership. It is important to be aware of the problem and acknowledge it the way it is, but that is where the role of the imaginative images of the mind stops. Let the images brought to you by your imagination steer you to the possible solutions.

Solution providers make inspirational leaders.

The episode I mention here reaffirms the need to be solution-oriented in order to be an inspirational leader. Once, an incident occurred in a school causing chaos, making matters abominably dangerous due to some folly and poor leadership. I was assigned the task of addressing the problem. Everybody around me imagined terrible results and worried that either the school would be shut down or we would get into a long-drawn-out battle between parents and the management. I imagined otherwise. I knew that the loophole could be plugged. Imagination took over, solutions emerged, and there I was with positive steps and meaningful solutions. Without ever submitting to any pressure, the problem was solved, and teaching remained in progress throughout. Here, I attribute my accomplishment to my imagining of handling the crisis as a bubble and not a catastrophe.

The first step to leadership is being able to lead your life through every problem, and then step out to solve problems at larger levels, each time going notches higher. Let the power of your imagination lead the way.

Leadership is about allowing your imagination to help you achieve goals, which may be small tasks, or magnificent goals that include invention and exploration.

Imagination gives fuel to the fire of creativity and innovation. However, at times, you may feel that your imagination is not as active as you wish it to be. With practice comes perfection. Every leader, across all walks of life, has spoken about the need for practice and discipline.

Practise ways to calm the mind and silence the confusions within, in order to allow imagination to have contact with the mind.

Discipline the mind in order to practise regularly, so that the mind is sound, which will allow your imagination and inventions to present themselves, as and when required.

There are times when the imagination may not be as active as it should be. However, by practising certain techniques, you can help your mind to activate the faculty of imagination to help you become an impressive leader.

These techniques can be practised and perfected as follows:

1. Every day, choose a fixed time to sit down at your desk with your journal or a sheet of paper, along with colouring pencils or crayons, or even gel pens. Lay them all out in front of you. Then close your eyes and take a

few deep breaths to relax. Without opening your eyes, pick up any colour that your hand is led towards and scribble or draw lines on the paper. You can change the colour as often as you want. Do not open your eyes till you feel there is nothing else to add. Simply allow your imagination to create this picture, and feel as if your hand is being guided by your imagination and not by you. When you open your eyes, look at the picture and pen down all the thoughts that will flow effortlessly.

I find this method effective, as a daily practice, as well as when I feel the problem I need to deal with is overpowering my imagination. This process helps me find the solution guided by my imagination. Like Einstein said, "Knowledge is limited. Imagination encircles the world."

2. I love reading, especially autobiographies and biographies and other great works. However, I don't just read books; I study them in order to ignite my own imagination. I delve into understanding what could have brought the author to write that particular piece of literature, what emotions probably drove them to pen their story, what could be their inspiration and motivation, what insight are they offering the reader, what is the background of every character, what could they have possibly been doing before they were placed on the scene, and what could their future be after the book is completed. These thoughts help me empower my own imagination, widening my scope

of understanding people. This is especially important for me because, as a principal, every day, I deal with children of all ages, and teachers and parents, amongst a lot of other people. I have had to take on the role of a trouble-shooter on the go. My imagination needs to be accelerating in full gear, so that it can guide me to intuit as well as understand the person and the problem, as a character from my book of life. Thus, empowering my imagination makes me empathetic, rather than sympathetic, and respected.

3. I feel my imagination is all the more empowered because I am always awestruck by all that I see around me, especially in nature. When I take a walk in nature, I observe all that I can, question in wonderment the "how" of it all. In fact, every vacation of mine is like an exploration into nature, as well as the wonders of the urban jungles. While nature constructs itself, genius imaginations have created some of the unfathomable wonders of the cities around the world.

I have a friend from the acting fraternity who told me about an interesting game she learnt in acting school, which has helped her perform well, as it takes her to depths of understanding the character better. I do indulge in this game when I feel I am stuck and my imagination is feeling too lazy. Imagination is always motivated by a good game! "Yes and so … No, but why" and "Because this happened … that happened … because that happened …" This mental stack game opens the doors to the imagination to bring in ideas and solutions, possibilities and probabilities. The more you practise it, the more original ideas flow, and the faster the solutions come.

Act, now! I believe that whatever comes to mind, act upon it now. That does not mean if your mind says, "Let's go to Japan", you pack your bags and head to the airport, without a visa. It means that when your imagination prompts you to be proactive, when it comes up with solutions that require you to take initiative, act now! It is all about making notes of the prompts provided to you by your imagination. Let these prompts mark the road map to your goal. This works like magic, as I have seen solutions falling into place and doors opening to show me the direction to my goals. However, do not just sit on the prompts; act upon them, as you deem fit.

Denis Waitley says it well, "You have all the reason in the world to achieve your grandest dreams. Imagination plus innovation equals realisation."

According to George Bernard Shaw, "Imagination is the beginning of creation. You imagine what you desire, you will what you imagine, and at last, you create what you will."

To sum up the importance of the faculty of Imagination, I have learnt:

"Wise thoughts add fuel to the imagination that metamorphose into reality experiences. Imagine a dream destination, and the power of leadership within you is bound to land you there. Such is the power of all imaginative leaders."

3

INSIGHT

"I know of no single formula for success. But over the years I have observed that some attributes of leadership are universal and are often about finding ways of encouraging people to combine their efforts, their talents, their insights, their enthusiasm and their inspiration to work together."

— Queen Elizabeth II

While imagination presents pictures to the mind, insight is the faculty of the mind to comprehend what messages these images carry. To be an effective leader, it is not just enough to know the images reflected upon the mind by the imagination; one needs to go to the depths of understanding what they nudge you to know.

The word 'insight' finds its roots in the ancient English word *innsihht*, circa 1200. *Innsihht* was then noted to mean "sight with the 'eyes' of the mind; mental vision; understanding from within." This word was derived from combining the preposition *in* with *sight*. However, initially it was felt that this word means 'sight into,' which gave the word a different connotation, and so for a long time it came to be regarded as the 'penetrating understanding into character or hidden nature,' circa 1580. Eventually, the word 'insight' came to be defined as, a clear, deep, and sometimes sudden understanding of a complicated problem or situation, or the ability to have such an understanding.

In accordance with my understanding, insight is a relevant parameter to lead oneself. Unless you have an understanding of what you are doing, there is not much that you can actually achieve. Have you ever noticed how dogs keep chasing their tails? They have no reason or understanding, but only possibly for the pleasure of the activity or out of sheer frustration, they simply chase their tails till they tire themselves out.

Without a sharpened ability to look within and go into the depths of understanding the images the imagination projects on your mind, you will be constantly working on manifesting those images into a reality, but to no avail; or you may just allow those images to entertain you through the day, leading you to indulge in day-dreaming and laziness.

While the word 'insight' has many synonyms, I feel that the following anecdote will be able to explain this word to you best.

There was a school reunion of a batch of ex-students. This was hosted by an old teacher of the school, who was in his eighties. He was leading a serene retired life.

The evening was spent in exchanging notes with each other about life and journeys; some shared their successes, some laughed about their failures.

The professor requested all the ex-students to hand over their visiting cards as they entered. There were lawyers, doctors, scientists, etc. Surprisingly, none had achieved a degree less than that of a post-graduate, and none were unemployed. This made the professor rather proud of the entire batch.

As each student gave their card, the professor handed his to them. His visiting card read, B.Sc., B.Ed., which were degrees of yesteryears' benchmark, indicating one was highly educated. However, considering his degrees at present, they were definitely ahead of him in the degree race.

He, however, felt honoured having met them all. His heart swelled with pride, because all his students had taken large strides in their lives. It did not matter that his students had not kept in touch after they completed their schooling. He knew in his heart he had given his students wings to fly upwards and beyond, rather than downwards.

Before the end of the evening, he delivered an inspiring speech: "Give wings to as many as you can. In whatever you do for them, you become more powerful and stronger when the birds come back to touch your heart, and then go forth to their flying, just like you all have done."

His speech was well-received with a thunderous standing ovation. A message that touched each one's heart, inspiring them to go all out and make their mark, inspiring more leaders in the making.

This is an insightful leader, one who understands in-depth why his students were not able to be in touch with him all these years. He did not lament their lack of contact with him; rather he celebrated their journeys. He rose in their eyes that evening.

Human Resource is the greatest resource of all.

When I was put in charge of a huge staff and young students, my challenge lay in understanding the staff, rather than the students. It was easy to gain insights about the students and lead them towards their goals; but when it came to the staff, it was far more tedious to get an insight into their lives and their mindset. I would often write the name of a staff member and doodle them or make notes as they reflected in my imagination, and then pen what would be coming forth. Based on these notes, I would call the staff members to my office, gain their confidence and then start discussions based on what I gathered could be their problem/s. I was astonished by the accuracy of the insights that were gained from this exercise. The teachers trusted me all the more and steadily, I could develop a team of inspiring teachers, always motivated to bring out the best in their students.

I must reveal that it never really mattered how accurate the insight was, because nonetheless, the exercise of digging deep for insights always helped me break the ice with the staff members, understand them better and help them resolve issues that were blocking them from being effective and efficient teachers who would create leaders amongst their students.

After all, discernment to see what others cannot, when it comes to those under your care, is an art.

I feel that delving deep for insights makes one even more patient and empathetic as a leader.

To define insight as easily as possible, I have read many experts who state it is the 'Aha!' moment, but for me, this is my 'I got it!' moment. It is the moment when the solution to a problem arises from the inner depth of your being. While for many the code word is 'Aha!', for Archimedes it was "Eureka!", for me it is 'I got it!'

The 'I got it' moment does not occur out of the blue, without a precedence attached to it. The fact is that there are repetitions and patterns, practice, study, research and discipline that precede that golden moment. Yet, it does not occur when you are preoccupied with the problem. It happens when you look at the other side and allow the insight to flood you. It is important to be aware and yet receptive and open, in order to utilise your insights effectively.

Leaders from different walks of life have experienced their moments of insight when they have least expected them. The idea is not to obsess about the problem beyond the point of having gone to the root of the problem. After that, continue doing what you need to; and then, just like that, as you observe every aspect of your day, the solution shall come to you.

Steve Jobs claimed, "If you define the problem correctly, you almost have the solution."

Just like when I doodled and created random character and personality sketches of the members of the staff, my 'I got it!' moment occurred when realisation dawned that each doodle and written sketch was unique and definitely different from each other. This brought to me the master plan: "Speak to each staff member separately to understand them deeply; not as my staff, but as human beings with a story. Befriend them, and lead them to understand themselves better, thereby empowering them to become effective teachers, not just explaining academic lessons to students, but also inspiring their students to keep improving, to achieve each day better versions of themselves."

The 'I got it' moment is not just about that one big insight that probably led Steve Jobs to create Apple, or Jan Koum to bring about WhatsApp, or Brad Pitt to become one of the best actors of Hollywood; but it is also about gaining insights to solve even day-to-day issues effectively. Great leaders, across walks of life, use their faculty of insight to help them lead their lives in ways that inspire others to also gain the courage to lead their own lives beyond horizons, scaling new heights.

Sara Blakely started out in sales and though she liked the support of pantyhose, she hated the way it looked with open-toed shoes. Her 'I got it!' moment came when she realised she could cut the "feet" off the pantyhose and work on redesigning the women's undergarment to create Spanx. That little idea of hers ballooned into a multimillion-dollar business, making her the youngest self-made female billionaire on the planet in 2012!

Bangalore-based Phanindra Sama wanted to travel to his hometown in Hyderabad once, and there were no bus seats available. That was his 'I got it' moment, when he got the insight to co-found Red Bus, an online bus ticketing start-up, which he sold to Ibibo for US $100 million.

Sarah Boone was one of the first African-American women to receive a patent in the US. Her imagination and insights led her to invent the modern ironing board in 1892. Boone's design comprised a wooden board which was narrow, had a padded cover and legs that could fold in. It was designed as a foldable, compact board that could be kept in a closet after use. In her patent application she wrote that the purpose of her invention was "… to produce a cheap, simple, convenient and highly effective device, particularly adapted to be used in ironing the sleeves and bodices of ladies' garments." Before her creation was introduced, people used to iron their clothes over a table or on a plank laid across two chairs.

In order to understand the meaning of insight, one needs to know the difference between insight and imagination. Primarily, imagination implies the images reflected upon the mind. Insight is the thought that gives us an understanding of the images reflected upon the mind, and also provides us solutions, inspired by the imagination.

While experts through time have provided an explanation for many types of thoughts, here, for the purpose of explaining insight, I am differentiating thoughts into those stored in the memory bank of the mind, and the fresh thoughts that occur. The memory thoughts serve as knowledge reserves, to help us effectively put fresh thoughts to productive use, or to discard, or alternatively, store those that do not serve a purpose at present.

Every insight is a fresh thought. However, not every fresh thought is converted into an insight. This is where the mind uses the ability to differentiate between the fresh thoughts as to which one is capable of providing an insight that could solve the problem at hand.

The story below will explain the technique of deriving and acting upon an insight.

In my years of teaching, I came across a student who was poor in studies and never showed any inkling towards making any effort. I needed an insight to help this grade 2 student, who lacked the zeal to study. While going through some documents, it suddenly dawned on me that I should understand the student's family background to know why he was so demotivated. This insight brought to me the revelation that his mother was a single parent, and the boy not only helped her with the household chores, but also spent most of the day alone while his mother worked. I urged his teachers to give him a little more attention, love and encouragement, and in the next couple of months, he showed improvement. He was filled with enthusiasm to participate in every activity.

Today, the same boy has grown into a successful man, standing tall and confident in the hospitality industry.

I feel satisfied that I could arrest the imbalance in his life in time, and help him mould a good career for himself.

According to the famous Dutch post-impressionist painter Vincent van Gogh, "If one is master of one thing and understands one thing well, one has at the same time, insight into and understanding of many things." I couldn't agree more! While most prefer being a Jack of many trades, I feel a master of one evolves one into becoming a King of all. This simply means that when you have in-depth insight into your subject of expertise, you eventually gain an understanding into a lot more. Your mind is open to explore farther and deeper; learn more and share more.

On the other hand, if the mind looks for insight into every fresh thought, there will be no achievement, except for exhaustion and fatigue that leads to frustration.

Accordingly, one should strive to be the greatest, by always seeking greatness in one; for mediocrity lies in the many, and genius in the one-pointed focused goal.

As a leader of my staff members and students, I am often inspired by the words of Dan Pena, founder of Quantum Leap Advantage, "Good leaders make sense of change in the world … then impart that insight to the team." While I do read a lot, and keep myself abreast with the news daily, I am often inspired by the changes I observe in nature. An important part of my daily routine is my walk in nature, where I observe all that is happening, gather the pictures in my mind, and become aware of the fresh thoughts they inspire. I then choose the productive fresh thoughts that serve as insights that can help solve nagging problems, be it my own—personal or professional—or problems faced by my loved ones, staff or students.

We gain powerful insights from observing nature. The touch-me-not plants always remain open; but the moment they confront stimuli touching, warming, blowing or shaking, they shrink and close as a defence from herbivores. Seeing this brought to me an insight: these sensitive plants close up in order to protect themselves from the vagaries of external elements. The botanist would probably think otherwise.

Just as imagination can become inactive, or the mind may not receive images from the imagination, so also fresh thoughts may not provide insights. In order to gain beneficial insights from the fresh thoughts, here are some activities that I have been using. They have been effective tools that have helped me gain insight into the solutions, while being aware of the problems.

MEDITATION: Calming the mind and silencing all the confusion, always helps me gain insight. I practise meditating for a minimum of 10 minutes every morning, and a minimum of 10 minutes every evening. While going to sleep at night, I meditate with the hope of gaining insight into any nagging problem. Most times I wake up in the morning with a solution, and I am good to go. Meditation is not being empty-minded and thoughtless. Instead, it is about being aware of your thoughts, feelings and sensations. It is being an observer of all that is happening. Here is guidance to the simple art of insightful meditation:

Sit or lie down comfortably. Close your eyes, and become aware of your breath. Observe the rhythm of inhalation and exhalation. As you relax, breathe deep and slow. When you are completely relaxed, in your mind, repeat three times, "I wish to seek insight into deciding on a career path." Then, observe your breath and the thoughts or visuals that come to mind (these thoughts or visions may be directly or indirectly linked to whatever insight you seek). As soon as you feel like surfacing back from your deep meditation, take another set of deep breaths and gently open your eyes. Then, on a sheet of paper, write or draw the thoughts that flow. The conclusion to your thought will be the insight you seek. Sometimes, you may need to meditate a few times, repeating the same process to gain a deeper insight. Sometimes, the insight may come at any point of the day.

As true as it can be, if an egg is broken by an outside force, then life ends. However, if broken by an inside force, life begins. Hence, great things always begin from the deep insight from within. Therefore, meditation can be considered as the base for the thought coming to life and attaining its universe.

DOODLING AND SCRIBBLING NOTES: One can gain insights from doodling and generally scribbling the random thoughts that keep coming into the mind through day-dreaming or generally thinking. These thoughts do have a purpose and/or meaning. However, one should try not to doodle or scribble mindlessly; instead, apply the thinking mind and make the exercise mindful.

Mindful insights are the mind's best teachers as they help it to learn where to look, but do not cloud the sight of the outcomes, and let it remain in the future's imagination and outcome. Hence, doodling helps the insights take life. And that life creates the journey.

PURSUE A HOBBY: When one is inundated by a problem, then one must indulge in an activity that distracts the mind from the nagging problem and relaxes it completely. This is the purpose of having a hobby. Reading helps me gain insights. I believe nothing is a coincidence, and all that happens is a chain of synchronicity. Sometimes, a line or paragraph or entire chapter gives me the insight into a problem.

WATCHING A MOVIE OR A PLAY: This can give one an insight to the problem, as certain movies can be similar to our life in the past, present or the future. Sometimes, the movies can make us realise the deeper meaning to our life. The movies can inspire and lead to a deep thought-changing insight.

I feel: *"A keen and astute insight into a daily problem helps a leader take risks and innovate."*

4

INTUITION

"Have the courage to follow your heart and intuition. They somehow already know what you truly want to become. Everything else is secondary."

— Steve Jobs

How true this is! This chapter takes you on a voyage into the deep blue sea where the rainbow manifests itself through your intuition.

The word 'intuition' stems from the Latin word *intueri*, which means to 'look at, consider'. *Intueri* comprises two words—'in' meaning 'at, on,' and *tueri*, which means 'to look at, watch over.' In later Latin, the word *intueri* took the form of intuitionem, which was listed as 'a looking at, consideration'. In the mid-15th century, it took the form of *intuicioun*, which came to denote, 'insight, direct or immediate cognition, spiritual perception.'

However, in its present form, the word 'intuition' was found in texts dating back to the end of the 15th century. Till the 17th century, the meaning of the word 'intuition' was listed as 'mentally looking at the act of regarding, examining or inspecting; a view, regard or consideration of something.' These meanings are considered obsolete at present.

The scholastic philosophers of the 17th century began to give the word a more spiritual connotation: 'a spiritual perception or immediate knowledge, ascribed to angels and spiritual beings, with whom vision and knowledge are identical.'

According to the Oxford Dictionary, 'intuition' means 'the ability to know something by using your feelings, rather than considering the facts', and also 'an idea or a strong feeling that something is true although you cannot explain why.'

Intuition is that first thought that comes to mind that seems to be a solution, a clue, a nudge, an inspiration, a warning. Thereafter, the second thought is what brings in confusion as it is a mindful thought; the third thought brings in judgements and biases, and stems from the ego, the 'I' of either inferiority or superiority. The 'I' that stems from thoughts may or may not be experience-driven; hence, these thoughts lack the innocence of the first thought.

To explain this, I would like to share an experiment I once conducted with a group of friends. For them, it was a game, but for me it was a test to deepen the roots of my understanding of the word 'intuition'.

A couple of years ago, a group of five of us, A, B, C, D and I, travelled to Africa for a safari. We were to stay at a wildlife sanctuary, in tents. It was an adventurous camping vacation. Such vacations always bring one closer to nature, and all the more take one into one's inner world. These moments lead the path to the insights into one's pure self. I am always inspired by wholesome rustic nature. I feel that is what teaches me every concept of not only being an effective leader, but a better being, with each passing day.

So, we were all sitting by the campfire that night and our guide told us that we needed to decide upon a leader. While my four friends pointed in my direction, I preferred to take a backseat and avoid taking on a leadership task as I wanted to be one with nature on my vacation. I strongly felt this was my opportunity to understand the importance of intuitiveness of a leader.

So, I suggested, "What if we do not choose a leader, and instead just go along together, each day as it comes?" Within a second, A said, "There will be confusion in times of urgency, so I suggest we pick a leader." After a few minutes, B appeared confused and said, "I am not sure whether we need a leader or not. I mean, if we have a leader, maybe it's fine, or maybe it's fine without a leader." A few minutes later, C spoke with a hint of irritation, "I think having a leader amongst us might just be a foolish idea, as well as extremely childish. We are five adults who don't need supervision. Silly idea!" D finally spoke from the space of inferiority, "I am not capable of leading.

A could lead, B could be an assistant leader, C could just follow along with me; and you (as in I) could be leader in the background."

I could see that B was confused, C was immersed in judging the situation, D was cowardly and trying to shy away from responsibilities. However, A was the quickest to respond with a solution.

While all this discussion was happening, A was involved in studying the itinerary for the next eight days, and was making his notes. His hand seemed to be writing as if in auto-pilot mode.

He was the only one amongst the five of us who instinctively took on the responsibility of being a leader and within 20 minutes, he had a map prepared for the adventures of the coming eight days.

Through that trip, A was the one who would instinctively guide us through the tough courses and terrains. His intuition guided him, while the others kept bickering about how difficult this trip was, because each one was either confused, judging or stuck in complexes. I walked along with A feeling secure and safe, knowing that no harm could come my way when I had a leader who followed his intuition.

On our way back, I asked A, "What makes you so sure of your intuition?" He promptly replied, "Every successful leader follows the lead of the first thought, for all the rest that follow fuel either confusion, judgements or discriminations. Leadership needs you to be on your toes—smart, light and quick!"

"Leadership is less about commanding and more about empowering people to live up to their potential by using all their abilities," he added.

I could not agree more! Leaders have to be great risk-takers in order to be successful. They depend a lot on their intuitiveness. That is why one often hears them say, "My gut feeling is that the road I take is surely the path to be followed."

While imagination brings images to the mind, insight is that Aha! moment, intuition is the feeling, instinct or gut revelation that helps you chalk out your road map to success. It is your sensitivity, sensibility and gracious awareness of your intuitions that help you mould yourself into an ultimate leader, inspiring others to walk your talk.

Intuitiveness is the use of the sixth sense that can help you become successful. Intuitive prowess comes with analysis and constant survey of the things around you. Somewhere, at some point, a leader-in-the-making becomes intuitive. It is a power that can be created within you if you dare to take up a task that you are sure will take you to the horizon of your vision. Leaders are capable of making effective decisions; they are not only able to listen to their gut feelings, but also obey them loyally.

Albert Einstein mentioned, "I believe in Intuition and Inspiration. I sometimes feel that I am right. I do not know that I am."

What he means is that you need to trust how and what you feel, over what you think or believe you know. The power of being a successful leader exists in the feeling that stems from the knowing, and not the knowing that creates an illusory feeling.

Let me simplify this with an example. Suppose you are travelling on a train and a co-passenger shows signs of uneasiness. You feel that this person needs some water and you immediately reach out with your bottle of water, and she is relieved. On the other hand, you ignore the feeling that nudges you to realise the emergency and instead start to think of what could be wrong with the person. You start thinking of solutions that are probably not within the immediate realm of possibilities. Well then, from being uneasy, this person could have lost consciousness and left you with immense guilt, because all that this person needed was some water!

Instructive leadership comes into existence using intuitive intelligence to guide decision-making.

Non-conscious processes operate not only in routine activities, but also in complex decision-making. Should one always go with one's gut instincts? As a leader, if you ask me, yes it always works, because all leaders are decision-makers. In times of dire necessity, intuitiveness is not just the best support, but actually the only.

Here is an exemplary true story about the value of being intuitive.

US Airways Emergency Landing

In 2009, Pilot Sullenberger, aka Sully, successfully landed his aircraft, US Airways flight 1549, in the Hudson River, when both engines in the airplane were incapacitated by a bird strike. This saved the lives of all passengers on board.

What made him take this decision? It was intuition alone. His gut told him to land in the water and he did exactly that, saving every life in that airplane.

Years of experience told him that he could do it. It was his gut feeling that spelt victory.

As a leader, taking the team through troubled waters requires a great amount of risk-taking and working on the 'gut feeling'. Luck isn't all about being at the right place at the right time. "Luck is when preparation meets opportunity," stated Seneca, the Roman Stoic philosopher.

Another story that explains why one needs to work on the language of one's intuition is about mountaineers Edmund Hillary and Tenzing Norgay.

On May 29, 1953, Edmund Hillary and Tenzing Norgay were the first to summit Mt. Everest, the highest peak in the world. The bee-keeper from New Zealand and the local Sherpa from Nepal were an unlikely duo to be the first to conquer the highest mountain. At the end of it, they remarked that success touched their feet as they made every decision during the daredevil summit following their intuition. They both went on to become role models for the mountaineering fraternity.

The ingredients of their intuitive planning were:

i)   Follow your heart
ii) Be alert and active
iii) Never despair. Stay positive.
iv) Be resilient. Bad turns to good. In every adversity, there is a blessing.

The mountaineers made their own luck. As Edmund Hillary would later write, "People do not decide to become extraordinary. They decide to accomplish extraordinary things."

If we look around, we will find that all creatures have the power of intuition. However, what makes you a master and a leader is when you hear the feelings within you, and are able to stride over dangerous terrain.

Practise listening to your intuition, your inner voice; ask questions, be curious, see what you see, hear what you hear, and then act upon what you know to be true. These intuitive powers were given to your soul when you were created. These will never fade away; they will remain infinitely, birth after birth.

Animals have this uncanny sense that warns of disasters. Animal behaviourists and biologists have observed that in the instance of earthquakes, animals can sense the disruption in the electromagnetic fields and announce, loudly and alarmingly, the impeding earth-shattering experience in that zone.

On 23 August 2011, at the Smithsonian's National Zoological Park in Washington DC, an orangutan named Iris let out a piercing guttural cry, which a primatologist termed as 'belch vocalising'. This cry startled the 300 zoo-keepers. They thought that perhaps some predator was afoot, or some other orangutan had threatened Iris. Instead, five seconds later, an earthquake measuring 5.8 on the Richter scale shook the city so badly that it damaged the Washington monument. Iris wasn't alone in forewarning the city. Sixty-four flamingos clustered together. Red lemurs set off an alarm cry 15 minutes before the calamity; a bull elephant warned the elephants in the pen, big cats paced nervously and the beloved reptile Murphy the Komodo dragon took cover.

All these tales of intuition and advocacy are lessons of leadership. So aptly runs the English folk rhyme:

> "When pigs carry sticks,
> The clouds will play tricks.
> When they lie in the mud,
> There are no fears of a flood."

Intuitive leaders are stoically wise and intelligent people.

Intuitive leaders are born from the unadulterated spirit, the true soul, not the 'I' of the ego. When in doubt, look within the subconscious mind. This does not mean you need to deny your own experiences and all that you have empirically learned through the years. It means to trust the inner unfiltered you and to integrate intuition, insights and experience. There is a balance, a harmony to be nurtured between the soul and the mind. When intuition rings clear and true, what the true self experiences, evolves to be the guided outcome, which filters to the ones who need to be led to become wholesome leaders.

I have been able to sharpen my awareness of intuition by concentrating on the laws of nature. I believe that almost all leaders, consciously or subconsciously, are inspired by nature when it comes to honing their ability to actually follow their intuition.

Whenever I conduct interviews to employ teachers, I recruit them based on what my intuitiveness says to me.

The goal of any leader is to help individuals grow so that the institution grows. Whenever the individual transgresses, personal growth takes precedence over the growth of the institution. When I sense this in my institution, I take action accordingly. One can call it experience, or intuition. Here, I would like to state that experience leads to intuitive sensitivity and sensibility. Having a wealth of experience to draw from is one of the key factors of being intuitive leaders.

Intuitive leaders are not what we call street-smart. It is a rather crude way of describing the effective leader who is spontaneous and instinctive.

Intuitive leaders never fall into a SOUP, for they are:

i)   Sensitive to their feelings
ii) Optimistic, and do not allow negativity to overpower them
iii) Unassuming, and understanding
iv) Persistent, and passionate about their work

Developing Sherlock Holmes' 'gut feeling' methodology helps all leaders make quick decisions. It is done by:

i)   Concentrating/meditating on a thought
ii) Sharpening your senses
iii) Observing
iv) Analysing
v)   Reflecting

Intuition means exactly what it sounds like, in-tuition. An inner tutor is like an intangible teaching and learning mechanism that takes us forward to achieve all our desired goals. It is a resource that was recognised to generate infinite potential amongst all living beings.

Comprehending your intuitive thoughts is essential on your journey of personal transformation and leadership. Intuition connects you with your soul, and this connection gives you access to your sixth sense, your heartfelt desires, your integrity and the inspiration you would like to acquire to be an effective and efficient leader, who will lead by setting an example, and also create many more leaders in the expedition of existence.

According to Robert Graves, "Intuition is the supra-logic that cuts out all the routine processes of thought and leaps straight from the problem to the answer."

Dogs have a great sense of intuition. I have personally experienced this many a time with my dog Brutus. He knows exactly what time I would be returning from work and waits near the door to receive me. Most of the time, the return has been as per my daily schedule. However, even on days when I am later or earlier than my scheduled time, Brutus waits at the door, promptly sensing my arrival.

Horses are known to neigh fiercely when they sense impending danger.

Much as we know that an intuitive intellect helps one make rapid-action judgements and decisions, I have experienced that an intuitive mind directs one's heart to make sensible decisions.

If psychologists call it (intuition) immediate understanding, knowledge or awareness, derived neither from perception nor from reasoning, scientists call it the subconscious way of operating. I realise that if I have become a leader, it has been my sensitivity to intuitive thoughts that has enriched my progress as a leader.

Oprah Winfrey rightly said, "Follow your instincts. That's where true wisdom manifests itself."

I knew of a friend who was considering leaving her job, but could not make a final decision. She did not want to take a step she would regret. She had gone through every analytical exercise she could think of, such as pros/cons list, talking to family members, friends, as well as envisioning what it would be like if she continued versus if she left the job. While out shopping one day, the intuitive sense got the better of her and signalled that a change of job was a must if further dreams were to be manifested. She could hear herself exclaim 'Yes' to this thought. At that moment, she decided to resign from the job. The theoretical mind was overtaken by actionable sense. Today, she is a Director of a big educational organisation, and making decisions is an easy task for her.

These exercises will help you develop your sensitivity to your intuitions; being one with them. It will help you comprehend the codes.

Intuition uses the senses to describe or receive information and knowledge.

A DATE WITH YOUR INTUITIVE SELF

Mark a two/three-hour date with yourself, on the calendar. When you go on this date with yourself, commence your journey, leaving your home or office with no plan or place in mind. You can walk, cycle, drive your car, use whatever mode of transport is available; you must be by yourself.

Resist the first few 'ideas' you have about where you are going. Wait for the idea that makes your thoughts and your body very relaxed. Your body is your best barometer of what is right—if your choice arises from intuition, you will experience inner stillness, silence and 'knowing' that it is right.

When the barometer is correct, go visit the person, place or event that intuitively comes to you. Then, once you are home and ready to go to bed, when you are two minutes away from going to sleep, revisit the time you commenced your journey to the time it was done. You will realise that the entire plan was orchestrated; it came from within—the inner self. The intuition gave you an experience you longed for. Only, this time, the intuition was the vehicle.

WORK WITH DREAMS AND ALTERED STATES OF THE MIND

Before you go to bed at night or lie down to rest during the day, place a pen and paper next to your bedside. After you lie down, mentally ask your intuition for a dream, or day-dream images that will benefit your life and the lives of those around you. Repeat your request as often as possible, before you drift off to sleep. When you wake up, even if you don't remember anything specific, write or draw whatever comes to your mind. Look over and evaluate what you receive. Act on the advice where appropriate action is required. This will lead you to scale greater heights in your life.

LOOK FOR SPECIFIC MESSAGES IN BOOKS OR MUSIC

Before you start your day, or when you're looking for a solution to a problem or issue, open a book—any book you're guided to—turn to any page, and read the paragraph upon which your sight rests. Let that paragraph be your guidance.

You can also do this with music. Set the intention that the next song you hear on your radio or iPod shall contain the guidance you need to hear. And then pay attention! The signs will most certainly come through.

Remember that the path taken in life is bound to be full of speed breakers; and a slowdown with a smooth ride over the bumps can help speed up the onward journey.

I feel the best way to conclude this chapter is with the following words by Jonas Salk:

"It is always with excitement that I wake up in the morning wondering what my intuition will toss up to me, like gifts from the sea. I work with it and rely on it. It's my partner."

5

INNOCENCE

"The greater our innocence, the greater our strength and the swifter our victory."

— Mahatma Gandhi

The word 'innocence' found its way into the English vocabulary from its Latin roots in the form of the word *innocentia*, meaning 'blamelessness, uprightness, integrity'. It stemmed into the old French word innocence, 'purity, chastity'. In the mid-14th century, the first use of the word in English was found in texts. Back then it was listed to mean, 'freedom from guilt or moral wrong'.

While glancing through the dictionary for a word, I found an interesting definition to one of the present day meanings of innocence: 'the quality of having no experience or knowledge of the more complex or unpleasant aspects of life'.

This ruffled the feathers of my mind and stuck with me for a long time, as I noticed the innocence with which innocent ants would industriously march each day to build their homes, or the queen bee would lead the entire colony to build a flourishing hive. Each creature seems untouched by the cruelties around and works towards accomplishing its goals, with a focus on its aims. The negative cannot bother them, as optimism makes them not only look forward, but march forward elegantly.

They do not allow their failures to affect their productivity. In fact, with child-like innocence, they look at their failures as stories that teach them important lessons. They take these lessons and work around them to create their successful missions.

This is the core of innocence—being untouched by the negative! This is an important aspect of ideal leadership.

> "The X factor of great leadership is not personality, it's humility."
>
> —Jim Collins

Effective leaders, who have a fertile imagination, gain insight and receive intuitive messages that they listen to. Yet, it is their innocence that fuels their optimistic, spontaneous actions and decisions that script their success stories.

Gandhiji once said, "The greatest lessons in life, if we would but stoop and humble ourselves, we would learn not from the grown-up learned men, but from so-called ignorant children." If the childlike wonderment, playfulness and excitement is lost, then the leader is considered to be dull and boring. This dull and boring leader may be looked up to with awe and respect, but one would definitely avoid spending any time with them, leave aside being inspired by them.

Innocence is a gift of inspirational, ideal leaders.

Every leader, to be effective, needs to make a little allowance for informal conversation with intelligent and ready, witty replies.

As a leader, you need to always ask yourself: "How can I do things in a better way?" It's important to kindle the spirit of curiosity, like in a child.

It is the innocence in us that brings in the creativity. Learning is a lifelong process. As a teacher previously, and now as principal, I know I could never have all the answers. I have never shied away from, nor admonished students, who would raise their hands and ask me a question for which I, at that time, would have no answer. In fact, I would make a note of the question and humbly, with a big smile, say that I would definitely look into the question and search for the answer, and also encourage all in the class to do so. In the next class, most of the students, including me, would return enthusiastically to share all the knowledge we found regarding the question at hand.

This is what I encourage every teacher to do, as more knowledge increases the thirst for even more. Leaders solve problems by searching for solutions, either from the depths of their experience, or knowledge troves.

Learning something new can be so much fun, and sharing that newfound knowledge is empowering!

Innocence is the child-like curiosity, adaptability and the capability to forget wrongdoings.

The ingredient of innocence in the 'I' of leadership involves hobbies, playtime and activities that actually bring all together, especially where team-building is concerned. It helps generate creativity, commitment, responsibility, trust, motivation, effective communication, flexibility and adaptability.

Another aspect of innocence that has stuck with me is 'wonderment'. I am amazed to see how children are wonderstruck by anything new given to them, be it a toy, a puzzle, a project. They go so deep into it to discover it, that they fuel their imagination to create something new. This is an important ingredient for leaders. Surely, every discoverer and inventor used the power of wonderment to industriously work towards inventing and discovering what their imagination triggered them to achieve.

According to the great philosopher Socrates, "Wonder is the beginning of wisdom." I believe every great leader is filled with the fire of wonder ignited by their imagination, insight and intuition. Solving problems effectively becomes their mission. Obstacles and failure on their way become the stepping stones to their peaks.

In fact, in the last couple of years, most global companies, especially the biggest IT companies, have incorporated gyms and recreational activity areas to motivate employees, allowing them fun breaks, which actually increases their productivity and reduces their stress levels.

There is a very fine line between childlike innocence and being childish.

Childlike innocence is backed by positivity and trust. Being childish is being immature and negative. A childish leader can never last long, but a childlike leader is remembered and cherished by all.

Amongst my teaching staff, I found that the successful and popular ones are the ones who are childlike; full of energy, maintaining the tenor of enthusiasm and curiosity. Every teacher needs to be in sync with every student, in order to bring out the best in them.

Another aspect of innocence, especially where leadership is concerned, is humility. The beauty of every child is their natural humility and respect for all. Till date, I seek inspiration from a line from Abraham Lincoln's letter to his son's teacher: "Steer him away from envy, if you can, teach him the secret of quiet laughter." He placed the teacher above himself. This, is humility personified. Unless leaders are humble, their ears would be shut to the probability of good counsel from others around to help them build and maintain their ventures.

Successful leaders do have a tendency to become bashful and insensitive when success meets them in the initial stages of their climb to their peaks. This actually leads to setbacks, and when they return to humility and to their ascent, it is like an escalator to the peak they summit.

I have found that innocence in leadership trains you to wear the important CAP of being a leader:

COLLABORATION: A leader is comfortable being one amongst the pack, as much as they enjoy the power of leading the pack. When you are one amongst all, you are aware of each one's strengths and weaknesses. It is often said that a leader is as strong as the team. If one believes that one can lead while being inconsiderate to the needs of others, then they shall be following their destiny to failure. Every great venture runs on the principle of collaborative effort put in by every team member, from the lowest to the highest rung, across all horizontals. Stubbornness and rigidity stunt progress. Enthusiasm nurtures creativity, which escalates enterprises to their peaks of success.

APPRECIATION: I always have non-prize winners also attend school functions, as one can learn to appreciate others. The capacity to praise and appreciate others opens up the mind to look at opportunities in every possibility.

PHILANTHROPY: If we don't learn to share, then we can never realise the joy of giving. Every leader not only imparts, but also shares, as it is a sure way to move upwards.

One can lead with innocent humility. Ideal inspirational leaders use simplicity and innocence as weapons while working towards moving from being good to becoming great.

Simple and humble leaders are more approachable, and it is fun to have them around. When I met Mr JRD Tata at a wedding ceremony, I was so in awe of him that I kept praising him for all that he did for the country. He asked me, "What do you do for a living?" I replied, "I'm a teacher." Almost spontaneously he replied, "You are great, for you are in a profession that moulds all of us." He said this with a twinkle of innocence in his eyes. I was overwhelmed. This speaks hugely of his simplicity and large-heartedness.

The day we start counting our glories and awards, we lose our innocence, peace and the path to progress. Innocent leaders do not chase accolades; instead they walk along with you, inspiring you, just as they are inspired by you.

I feel that nurturing a childlike innocence is a lifelong process. I have found that the following activities help me connect with my innocence, especially when I feel overpowered by stress and fatigue. Or when I have to deal with a problem that does not seem to have an immediate solution in the line of vision.

SPORT is one way of creating balance of mind and gracefully accepting defeat, while learning how to congratulate the winners. Sports at any age reduces stress and enhances one's mood, increases fitness, improves sleep, helps socialisation, improves cooperation skills, boosts self-confidence and lowers the risk of getting obese.

There are many world leaders who played various sports in their spare time.

Barack Obama plays basketball, Donald Trump and the late Kim Jong Il play golf, Fidel Castro was a passionate baseball player, George W Bush was great at bowling, Prince Albert II of Monaco loved bobsledding; Princes Charles, William and Harry enjoy polo; Richard Nixon enjoyed bowling, Vladimir Putin plays hockey. These are examples of world leaders who spent their leisure time pursuing sports to destress and refuel to deal with their challenges.

TRAVEL is like food for thought. It changes one's perception towards life. It teaches you things that are beyond books, the internet, etc. It teaches you how to live wholesome.

Not only does travelling educate you on facts and trivia about a place, it also helps in your moral and mental growth. Studies have found that people who have travelled to different places since childhood are more likely to be open-minded and accepting. Socially, they are less likely to be racist and liberal. It's best that parents encourage children to travel in order to inculcate good values in them.

Travelling helps detox the mind and body. It also improves one's problem-solving skills that play a major role when exploring new places and situations.

Travelling is as inevitable as breathing. When you travel, you turn into a refined and intellectual person. You find yourself. It's like a spiritual healing, opening yourself up to the universe.

Here are five evidence-backed ways travelling makes your mind happy and healthy:

1. It's a great stress-buster.
2. It helps you reinvent yourself. Writer Patrick Rothfuss said, "A long stretch of road can teach you more about yourself than a hundred years of quietude."
3. It boosts happiness and satisfaction.
4. It makes you mentally resilient.
5. It enhances creativity.

SHARE YOUR TIME AND TALENT

All of us are blessed with talents, and good leaders find ways to share theirs, without the thought of getting anything in return. It's a small lesson you can take from those children you see sharing their toys or helping one another out of the goodness of their heart.

Here's a three-step process you can follow:

1. IDENTIFY your talent or how you would like to volunteer your time. Choose something you would do out of sheer love; it helps to pick something you are most passionate about.
2. INTEGRATE this with an individual's or a group's specific needs, because you need to have a relevant outlet for your endeavours. See how you can encourage and uplift, not just entertain or give directions from the sidelines.
3. INCULCATE this into your weekly routine, give it a meaningful length of time and stay true to your commitment.

You know best where your contribution can have the most impact. So, make a concrete decision about how and where you would like to volunteer your services. And get set to experience the joy that comes from enriching others, as well as yourself in the process.

Another way you can help is by "paying it forward". It's the opposite of paying back someone for a good deed done to you. Paying it forward happens when you perform an act of kindness for someone, and they in turn go out and help others, creating a chain of good deeds. You may never know the impact your good deed has had, but it's nice to set off a ripple effect of kindness.

Some simple examples: Giving up your seat in the bus to a tired commuter can help her relax physically and mentally before she gets home to prepare her family's favourite dish. Calling up a relative or friend you haven't been in touch with for a long time can uplift them in a special way. Keep a bowl of water out for the birds in summer months and they'll thank you in their own melodic way. The opportunities could crop up at any moment during your day, so make the most of them.

There is a Chinese saying that goes: "If you want happiness for an hour, take a nap. If you want happiness for a day, go fishing. If you want happiness for a year, inherit a fortune. If you want happiness for a lifetime, help somebody." For centuries, the greatest thinkers have suggested the same thing: Happiness is found in helping others.

According to Charles Duback, "Enlightenment takes place when one lets his innocence emerge and sees nature and life with a childlike awe and respect."

Here are some activities that you can incorporate to

ensure your childlike enthusiasm is not watered down by stress, to become an excellent leader:

1. Spend a minimum of 20 minutes each day doing something you enjoy a lot. It could be solving a crossword, reading a book, gardening, going for a walk. It can be any activity that brings you closest to your childlike innocence.
2. Learn something new every day. Take up a subject you are passionate about, and different from what you do as a routine. For instance, you can try out a new recipe every day, or learn a new word or idiom, or read an article that gives you information on a topic you enjoy exploring, like astronomy, geography, etc. An expanded mind is a childlike, happy mind.

In conclusion, I believe that we need to learn to be sufficiently humble to seek help for problems we cannot solve, as we cannot hope to be the best at everything. The sooner one realises this, the greater is the success as a leader.

6

INDUSTRIOUSNESS

"I was obliged to be industrious. Whoever is equally industrious will succeed equally well."

— Johann Sebastian Bach

The root of the English word 'industrious' is the Latin word, *industria*—'diligence, industry'. It took the form of the word *industriosus*—'diligent, active, industrious'. It then went on to take the form of *industrieux* in the Mid-French era, before it was used in English in the 1550s, as the modern-day word 'industrious'. Back then, it was defined as 'characterised by energy, effort and attention; marked by industry'.

Present-day experts, who define an individual as being industrious, indicate it to mean that the person is hardworking, dedicated and a problem-solver.

While children get bored of their toys and games, or

whatever tasks are given to them, for ideal leaders, who are in touch with their childlike innocence, industriousness is one of their most important qualities. Leaders are prepared to not only go back to the same task repeatedly, maintaining their enthusiasm, but are also ready to put in qualitative hours of proactive work to achieve their goals.

Industrious leaders work energetically, diligently and resourcefully.

For them, an obstacle fuels their energy to go all out, diligently looking, researching and experimenting with resources to solve any kind of problem. They are not unrealistic, but believe in focused, hard work, untiringly. Once they get going, they are on the go till they achieve their goals, and then look beyond, setting new aims.

> "Never tell people how to do things. Tell them what to do and they will surprise you with their ingenuity."
> —General George Patton

Industrious leaders are not just active, they are proactive leaders. Every time I think of industriousness and leadership, I am reminded of the Aesop's fable of 'The Ant and the Grasshopper'.

The grasshopper always teased the ant about his dull and monotonous life, while he himself indulged in relaxed sunbathing all the time. However, when winter set in, the grasshopper died of hunger, as he had not stocked up any food, whereas the ant had industriously filled his coffers with food, while the sun shone. The ant was always aware of the severity of the winters, which would not allow him to venture out for food. He knew if he worked through the entire summer, then he could relax and enjoy the harsh winter in the warmth of his anthill. He inspired all to follow suit, so that the entire colony survived the winters, as they waited patiently for the warmth of the spring sunshine, to set forth to industriously work again.

Every ideal leader follows a strong work ethic. People tend to believe that leaders do nothing more than delegate, or oversee their entire project, enterprise or mission. The fact is that they all have a strong base, rooted in hard work that is constant and consistent. They know the ropes of every aspect of their venture, so when they reach the top, they understand every aspect of the level. They know how to solve every problem, in every department.

> "Men make history and not the other way around. In periods where there is no leadership, society stands still. Progress occurs when courageous, skilful leaders seize the opportunity to change things for the better."
>
> —Harry S Truman

Delegation for them is not simply about passing on a task, but actually providing an opportunity to those who are leaders in their own right. The ideal leader considers all team members to be leaders in their own space and pace. "With great power comes great responsibility," said Voltaire. The effective leader is aware of how vital it is to empower the entire team and encourage them to take responsibility, for human-power is the greatest resource for every organisation.

> "The most efficient way to live reasonably is every morning to make a plan of one's day and every night to examine the results obtained."
>
> —Alexis Carrel

I like what someone said to me once, "No matter how clever you are, what technologies you have, no strategy will help you attain success unless you are visible and taking action." Every successful star of every walk of life has made it big by working hard. Whatever profession you are in, constant upgrading, focus on work and passion to work combined together, should be your cornerstone.

Hard work is considered hard work, as long as every moment of work is driven towards earning meaningful results, rather than working hard, putting in hours aimlessly, without any drive and passion. It is not just the number of hours that one puts in, but the quality of efforts. The ideal industrious leader puts in efforts that are qualitative, being proactive and result-oriented. They are considered smart workers.

John F Kennedy once stated, "Every accomplishment starts with the decision to try."

I have come across two kinds of leaders: one who is Active and the other Proactive. The active leader deals with the ongoing situation and is present to act upon or get busy with the situation—a leader constantly working at his or her delegating and doing the task successfully. A proactive leader goes a step further in being more engaging and goes beyond a short-term task. They initiate and offer help to co-workers who are actually driven. I'm convinced of one thing; leaders have to be good drivers. They need to take care of the traffic signals as well as speed breakers. An active driver will just follow the instructions on boards; a proactive driver will foresee things and engage in finding new routes.

Sometimes I laugh, as I wonder why the world seems to be getting busier than ever. Are we busy doing productive work, or do we just consume time for the sake of it? It all seems like quality over quantity. This makes me mindful of my own level of industriousness. Therefore, I, like almost every ideal industrious leader I have known or read about, maintain a planner.

I spend 15 minutes every morning, while sipping my coffee, making a list of every task, in order of priority, from the most important to the least, and I note the time limits for each task; be it the daily tasks, or those that require my efforts over a period of time. This ensures I use every working moment of my day productively. I feel a sense of responsibility towards the hours we have from the time we wake up till the time we sleep.

Hard work without any concrete results is not hard work; it's useful time being wasted. The greatest quality of any hardworking leader is goal-driven work.

This is the way I plan my day, every day, including the weekends. I do skip doing this on vacations, as then it's all about leisure!

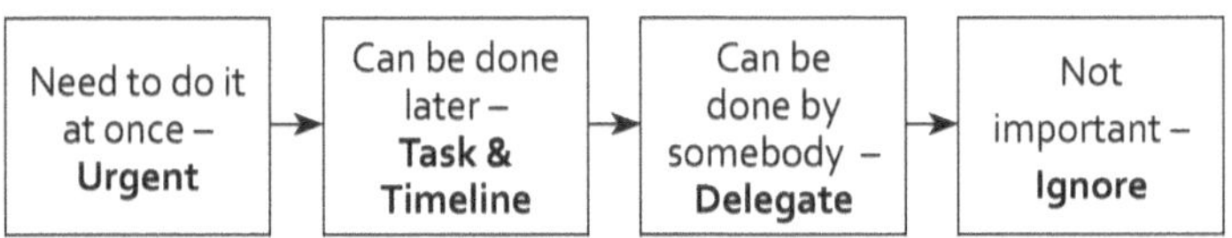

Learning how to prioritise work is an art. Based on the above task-chart, ideal industrious leaders know how to effectively ensure that they are being proactive. Work smart by utilising time to the maximum, rather than work hard. Leaders work smart and set a positive example of absolute result-oriented time with the utmost outcome.

1. URGENT implies all tasks that require to be done on a priority basis. There are no 'freebies' for the leader here. The goal is set and they have to micromanage, in order to complete the task. This generally happens when a sudden task comes your way, like a business deal that needs to be closed.

2. TASK AND TIMELINE implies all those tasks that can be postponed; however, they need to be earmarked for a specific deadline that needs to be followed in the near or distant future. This ensures the proactive leader is not stressed out about the said task before carrying it out to its completion, and that time can be spent strategising and planning.

3. DELEGATE implies all tasks that can be given to others to do, such as scheduling appointments, drafting documents, etc.

4. IGNORE implies all tasks that are unimportant, and do not need to be directly addressed by the leader, or where the leader's direct involvement is not required. While to an extent these tasks are delegated, they do not require any attention from the leader. For instance, planning the menu for a staff lunch meeting, or surfing the internet for information, etc.

I know, as a leader, one thing for sure: "Nothing is going to be given to me, just like that. There are no free lunches, raises, promotions, arrears, opportunities, etc., available freely. It has to be earned. What is earned through hard work always remains with oneself."

I know for sure, if I have earned glories in my profession, it is purely on the basis of merit and hard work. It is often said, there is no substitute for hard work. I tell my students, "To succeed, one cannot compromise on hard work."

I often remind myself of the following words by Zig Ziglar: "You were born to win, but to be a winner, you must plan to win, prepare to win, and expect to win." I know I have to strive to make productive use of each day in order to achieve higher and bigger goals; and all the more so that I ensure I lead by example, and not by merely preaching instructions to my students and teachers.

The ideal industrious leader has a clear EDGE over all others: Energy, Diligence, Genuineness and Earnestness towards their goals.

EDGE

a) ENERGY: To be industrious, one has to keep oneself young and energetic, and this can be attained only when the willingness to work is strong and one starts enjoying the task that needs to be completed.

b) DILIGENCE: I have not heard of any leader being successful without any dedication. Being dedicated to the task helps one become more focused and therefore, the goal can be easily attained.

c) GENUINENESS: Good work depends on being honest and ethical; superficial people only get short-lived success. Genuine leaders are remembered forever as their code of working principles is appreciated and is a benchmark for others to emulate.

d) EARNESTNESS: Being earnest implies being sincere and serious in all that one does. There should be an eagerness to work relentlessly and earnestly. I like Oscar Wilde, referring to *The Importance of Being Earnest* (a play), purporting that Victorian ideals were superficial and so it was necessary to be genuine and honest to oneself in all that is done.

I would like to share a little story I revisit each time I feel a little laziness begin to take over, especially when I return from my relaxed vacations. This story tends to inspire me.

There was a boy who joined a music class, as singing was his passion. No matter how well he sang, the master never praised him and made him sing again and again. While the other children went on to the next level, singing more difficult songs, the boy had to keep singing the same song. Three months passed by, yet the boy did not seem to attain the mark set by the master. The boy decided that during the upcoming vacations, he would keep practising so that by the time school started, he would be able to impress his master, enough to be promoted to the next level of singing.

On his way back home for the vacations, he dropped by at an inn for some refreshments. He saw a poster on the wall that *read: 'Music Competition Tonight—The best singer will win an award of $500. He decided to participate in the competition, and sing the same song that he had been practising for so many days. On the stage, not only was his voice sonorous, but every note was strung together melodiously and harmoniously too. He was awarded the first prize.*

When receiving the award, he spoke the following words in his gratitude speech:

"I owe this success to my music teacher, who made me practise this song to perfection. I worked extremely hard, never quitting, nor getting bored, even though I had to sing the same song, repeatedly."

Nothing comes without hard work. The freedom of India or any country would not have happened had the fighters not put in hard work, proactively.

> "The way to get started is to quit talking and begin doing."
>
> —Walt Disney

The below-mentioned activities will increase industriousness as well as time productivity.

1) THE GLASS JAR: This activity demonstrates the consequence of doing the most important tasks first.

You need: An empty, transparent, medium-sized glass jar, some large rocks, smaller rocks, gravel, sand and water.

What things you put into the glass jar first will determine how many of the other objects you can put in afterward.

Observation: If you put sand in first, nothing else will fit (except some water), but if you start with the big rocks (our most important tasks) and go down, you can fit some of everything in.

Hence, this activity helps us to prioritise time, work and effort according to the level of importance.

2) T3: You can overcome procrastination and discipline yourself to utilise time more efficiently and effectively with the Task Tracking Time—T3.

Does time seem to slip by each day and make you end up feeling that you didn't achieve what you wanted to achieve? One way to attack this problem is to keep track of your time using a simple time diary. Here is how it works…

1. Over the course of a few days, write down how you spent your time in a pocket note pad. Use shorthand like "e-mails: 10:00 am, 45 minutes for unscheduled visitor conversation: 2:15 pm, 55 minutes", etc.
2. At the end of each day, use highlighter pens to categorise your time:
   a) Red: expenditure of time that was non-essential
   b) Blue: expenditure of time that could or should have been shortened or tightened
   c) Yellow: expenditure of time that supported your work goals and objectives
3. Take a few minutes to assess your use of time. Answer the following questions:
   a) How did you feel about the day? Productive? Non-productive?

    b) What can I eliminate? Shorten? Or tighten?

    c) Do I spend too much time on non-essential tasks?

    d) Is my work focused on my priorities and goals?

    e) What tasks during the day frustrated me the most?

4. After a few days of tracking your time, identify one or two things that you are going to change to make your use of time more effective and goal focused.

Richard Branson said, "My general attitude to life is to enjoy every minute of every day. I never do anything with a feeling of, 'Oh God, I've got to do this today.'"

SIMPLE WAYS TO INCREASE INDUSTRIOUSNESS:

a) Decide to be productive/adopt a productivity mindset.

b) Prepare a to-do list and prioritise your tasks.

c) Block off time on your calendar/schedule and set earlier deadlines. Establish a daily routine and avoid distractions and time-wasters.

d) Break up big tasks into smaller components.

e) Monitor/measure your progress regularly.

f) Improve processes, efficiencies and tools.

g) Study and learn from other productive people.

h) Use your commute time to your benefit.

i) Create checklists.

j) Finish what you start.

k) Understand the big picture.

l) Improve your focus and concentration.

m) Practise risk management.

n) Reward yourself for accomplishing big goals.

"Yesterday is gone. Tomorrow has not yet come. We have only today. Let us begin."

—Mother Teresa

MOTHER TERESA symbolises charity, humility and empathy—she was a woman who reached out to the poorest of the poor. Why do we find her inspiring?

a)   For 'being the change' and showing us that all humans are meant to be treated equally.
b)   For proving that little acts of love and kindness can make an enormous difference.
c)   For her grace, wisdom and faith in the goodness of people.
d)   For leading by example and being a beacon of hope for the underprivileged.

I believe she is a wonderful example of how to live your life and I hope I can reflect the goodness she created for others in God's name.

"Be faithful in small things because it is in them that your strength lies."

—Mother Teresa

Some of the most inspirational, disciplined women athletes in India today, Sania Mirza, Saina Nehwal, PV Sindhu and Mary Kom have all been industrious and continue to play and win for one goal—that is India.

MARY KOM inspires me as she plays and wins against all odds with total determination and dedication. Truly, she is 'Magnificent Mary'. Mary Kom is a name that resonates patience and perseverance. A five-time world champion, Kom has battled far more than what we have seen her fight in the ring.

There are achievers and there are fighters. Mary Kom is both. Like many sportspersons in our country, from an amateur boxer who began her career in 2000 to a six-time world record holder, Mary Kom's fascinating journey has lessons for all. Mary Kom too was born in a poor family, and didn't have the best of education or resources to start a career. But what she had was the will to fight against all odds and an attitude to never give up.

"I want to dedicate the medal to all the people behind my hard work. I dedicate my gold medal to my nation," the world champion told the media after her triumph. Lessons that can be practised.

We have one more model who has mastered excellence in his profession and has the whole world at his feet—the music legend AR RAHMAN, who said, "When you do something with a lot of honesty, appetite and commitment, the input reflects in the output."

Almost thirty years have passed since Rahman's first release, *Roja*. Since then, he has become everybody's favourite. His list of numerous prestigious awards like the National Film Award, the Filmfare Award, the Padma Shri Award and the Oscar Award are evidence of his commendable success and excellence. He is a person whose focus has always been on excellence and this is what he has achieved all his life.

Today, AR Rahman is one of the world's most successful Indian musicians. With a brand name like Rahman, movies rake in millions. But it isn't just Rahman's exceptional enthusiasm that's so contagious, it's also the quality and success of the work he's churning out.

DR LH HIRANANDANI was the inspiration behind the edifice, Hiranandani Hospital. Under his stewardship, the ENT department attained vibrancy. The American Society of Head & Neck Surgery elected him as their first Indian member. He was the first Indian and the fifth in the world to receive the 'Golden Award' from the International Federation of Otolaryngology and Head & Neck Societies. In 2001, he received the 'ENT Surgeon of the Millennium Award' and the 'SAARC Award' on behalf of the SAARC countries. He was awarded the Maulana Azad Award '97 by the Indian National Congress in recognition of his exemplary work during the 1993 communal riots in Mumbai. In the field of medical ethics, he had spearheaded the passing of the Human Organs Transplantation Bill by the Lok Sabha in 1994. His humane nature made him stand up for the rights of people and fight against capital punishment and euthanasia.

In 1972, the Government of India awarded him the Padma Bhushan, the third highest civilian national award, for his contribution to the nation. In 1987, he was conferred the Dhanvantari Award, awarded for the first time in the field of ENT, for his notable contribution to medical science.

K SIVAN, the ISRO Chairman is an inspiration to many. Born to a farmer in Tarakkanvillai village in Kanyakumari district, he studied in a local government school.

Apart from being the ISRO chairman, Sivan was also appointed as the Secretary of the Department of Space and the Chair of the Space Commission. K Sivan assumed the role of ISRO chairman in January 2018. He is recognised for his contribution to the development of cryogenic engines and he has been a part of many projects including the Polar Satellite Launch Vehicle (PSLV) project.

As the clock kept ticking, all eyes were on the Indian Space Research Organisation (ISRO). Known as India's biggest space mission, besides being India's first-ever rover-based space mission to the Moon, Chandrayaan-2 was poised to be the world's first expedition to reach the Lunar south polar region.

The Project Director and Mission Director of the Rs. 978-crore Chandrayaan-2 mission are Muthayya Vanitha and Ritu Karidhal, both women scientists from ISRO, who are leading the country's space programmes. Also, it is noteworthy that 30 percent of the team leading Chandrayaan-2 are women.

> "The learnings from today will make us stronger and better; there will be a new dawn. The best is yet to come in our space programme; India is with you. Countless people have got access to a better life due to the hard work of our space scientists. Our determination to touch the moon has become even stronger, we came very close but we need to cover more ground,"
>
> —PM Narendra Modi

Luck visits those who are industrious. Proactive hard work always reaps magic and weaves success stories, for the world offers no free lunches unless you wish to stand in the queue for charity.

7

INVENTIVENESS

"I never did anything worth doing by accident, nor did any of my inventions come by accident; they came by work."

— Plato

Very often there is confusion between being innovative and being inventive. All leaders who are innovative need not be inventive and vice versa but the combination of being both inventive and innovative is deadly.

To be inventive is to be creative. Inventive people use their imagination and insights. What exactly is the meaning of the word 'inventive' and how is it different from innovation?

Invention is the creation of a new product for the first time, whereas innovation is bringing in a new dimension to the existing ideas. Leaders have already been inventive in labs, and sapiens, right from the Palaeolithic Age up to the present, had to be innovative. Necessity has always been the mother of invention but opportunity and thinking have led to innovation.

A simple lesson in history for a school child can be made interesting only by introducing innovative ways of teaching rather than by sticking to the inventive method. The lesson plan and methodology have been drafted and therefore I shall only stick to it. Why not say the plan and methodology have opened my mind to developing and adding more new ideas to the existing practices?

Invention is the creation of a product or the introduction of a process for the first time, like Thomas Edison inventing the bulb. Innovation is the improvement and contribution to an already existing thought like a motor vehicle.

A good leader is very practical and inventive. When a dire need for something arises, the leader becomes inventive.

For a school drama that had limited funds, the children had to make a number of props. Ideas poured in, when the principal decided to have a three-dimensional tent, to make a number of things like a cone, a tent, etc. This is inventive.

Leaders are watchful and observe keenly all things around them. In Shakespeare's play *Macbeth*, the prophecy "Great Birnam wood to high Dunsinane hill shall come" was not thought of, but Malcolm and his people covered themselves with tree branches and moved around in camouflage, which appeared as though the woods were moving. He was an inventive leader and hence, he won the battle against Macbeth.

Here are tests for—What is innovative and What is inventive?

Examples of Inventiveness: When students have project week symposiums and workshops, they make do with whatever is available. Team leaders extensively utilise resources while keeping waste management in mind. These are productive and inventive leaders.

Recycle, Reuse and Reduce is one of the finest examples of inventiveness. A leader who knows the three Rs is truly an inventive leader.

Come September, and in India, the Ganpati festival calls for a lot of Ganesha idols to be made. It is a symbol of worship and a must for praying. It is here that all the three Rs are used, and all those who follow the Reuse, Recycle and Reduce formula have been inventive. Eco-friendly Ganeshas are becoming more popular and their effect of reducing waste has increased phenomenally.

Likewise, all educators become inventive leaders the moment technology is brought into education. Inventiveness is nothing but the mantra—ICE.

I: Innovation through imagination

C: Creativity with limited resources

E: Exploration through various ideas and possibilities

It eventually leads to being ingenious. During the process, one becomes very clever and skilful. All artful and skilled leaders are inventive and ingenious.

Educators as leaders can cultivate inventiveness in children. One such way is the game 'Project Robinson Crusoe'.

Give a few things to students salvaged from a ship, creating a Robinson Crusoe simulation. They can pick up one of the items and explain how they would use it as an emergency life saver.

The students have to think out of the box and convince everyone that what he or she has picked up would be the exact straw of survival. Inventiveness can be seen on the sports field as well.

INVENTIVE MANTRA

If we reflect upon who are inventive leaders, we can see that anybody can be one. Here are a few examples:

a) The space crunch in offices and schools are combated by using the same space for multiple uses; for example, collapsible partitions in big rooms make more room to create several classrooms. This, I would say, is inventive.

b) An emergency and evacuation plan calls for presence of mind and being inventive. The one who is able to evacuate maximum people would have used inventive skills.

In academics, there are several examples of being inventive. A particular question in an examination can have different answers. A specific problem can be solved in several ways. Art and music in academics is a fine example of being inventive. All artists and musicians are talented people and inventive leaders.

TECHNOLOGY AND INVENTIVENESS

All scientists who came up with breakthrough ideas are inventive leaders. Today, there is a greater need for inventive leadership as it leads to production and manufacturing of more items. Inventiveness leads to creativity, leading to critical thinking. After all, Rome was not built in a day. A lot of inventive leaders had to apply their mind and put their thoughts together to bring up such a fine city while retaining its originality. The city has also succeeded in keeping up with the times by upgrading and through technological advancement.

If you want to tap the potential in individuals, never tell them how to do things. Tell them what to do, and they will surprise you with their ingenuity that calls for being inventive.

8

INNOVATIVENESS

"Innovation is taking two things that already exist and putting them together in a new way."

—Tom Freston

Someone had once said to me, "There is nothing original, actually; it's all definitely an inspired new version of something that was original during some era of existence." This helped me refine my understanding of the difference between 'being inventive' and 'being innovative'.

As we saw in the chapter on inventiveness, it is all about creating something new—bringing forth an invention. On the other hand, innovation is the renewal of something that has already existed. This is rather difficult, as an inventor has the pleasure of going down paths untrodden and discovering something new, unique, genuine. Conversely, the innovator has to creatively rehash what already exists, giving it a renewed breath of existence in a way that does not seem plagiarised, and is as good as new.

While many consider both inventiveness and innovativeness to be synonyms, I read an interesting article that differentiated between the two. The author mentioned that an inventive individual tends to "come up with many new ideas and concepts in many different situations". On the other hand, an innovative individual "will implement many new ideas ... creating a tangible impact upon his or other people's lives".

Can a leader be inventive and innovative? Yes, of course; as being one or the other depends on the purpose it serves. Does a leader have to be both inventive and innovative? I feel a complete leader should be able to be inventive when required and innovative, when innovativeness is called for.

As leaders, we have to keep thinking out of the box. The day we become complacent, believing that yesteryears' ideas still hold good, we will cease to grow. The world is dynamic and rapidly changing. Old resources are getting depleted and new ones are coming into existence. It is crucial for organisations to be innovative to stay competitive and ensure continued success.

As school leaders, we are always trying to initiate new programmes in the curriculum, as well as in the arena of extracurricular activities. We are dealing with iGen/GenZ bulk that is more informed, more creative and very inquisitive. The leadership to guide GenZ definitely places more importance on Innovation. Not that it did not exist earlier, but it is definitely getting more pronounced now.

We all know that a civics class can be brought alive by conducting role play and organising youth parliament sessions. And yet, we cannot ignore that the Model United Nations (MUN) sessions are a big catalyst to greater learning of global nuances. Furthermore, a leader also came up with a greater idea of calling it a 'Diplomathon', where diplomacy and communication skills are honed. All this is innovation—new ways of not just teaching, but also inspiring practical use of knowledge.

"I want to put a ding in the universe," said Steve Jobs, and thus was created Apple, which set off a revolution in microcomputers, the animated world, movies, music, phones, tablet computing and digital publishing. Once you set the ball rolling as a leader, all those who look up to you will look back at your achievement. They will see ahead, and will drive innovation to greater heights.

Innovation comes in when resources are few. It is the art of doing more, and better, with less.

I believe that, "If you want something new, you have to stop doing something old."

Innovation can help you reap profits beyond the profit you have the thought of manifesting.

> "If you look at history, innovation doesn't come from just giving people incentives; it comes from creating environments where their ideas can connect."
>
> —Steven Johnson

Here is a little story about two blind men:

Two blind men sat on a curb on the streets of New York, to earn some coins for their daily necessities. One of them wrote on a cardboard, 'I'm blind, I cannot see'. The other one wrote on his cardboard, 'Today is a Beautiful Day. I cannot see it'. This creative blind man, who wrote an innovative message on his cardboard, earned more coins than the one who wrote the simple words.

To be creative and look for a better way to do all that needs to be done makes a leader successful.

For almost all schools, games are played at the end of the day. I decided to change that, and introduced games in the first part of the day, followed by a short break. The teaching staff noticed that this made the students motivated, disciplined and even more energetic during their regular class sessions. Many schools have followed suit, and feel that it has helped to improve the academic performance of their students.

The quadrant below represents the four priorities of an innovative leader:

1	Strategic Vision	Creation of Trust and Faith	2
3	Emphasis on Speed and Follow-up	Inspiration and Motivation	4

As is rightly said about Mark Zuckerberg, "Young he may be, but his winning strategy of innovation was hiring passion over skill." Always consider giving people jobs they are passionate about; the best will come out of it and naturally the skill gets honed.

1. STRATEGIC VISION: An innovative leader must have a vision. Unless there is a road map indicating the path towards growth, the leader would be directionless. All leaders need to strategise a set vision. Ideal inspirational leaders have a clear and focused vision of what they aim to achieve. For example, every principal envisions that each student is moulded to be a lifelong learner, critical thinker and, above all, an ideal inspirational leader.

   As a leader, you need to have a vision of a fixed destination and goal. This takes the form of a statement encompassing all that you and your venture represents. For example, if my vision is to bring about all-round development in students, through academic and non-academic activities, then the mission would contain a few objectives and goals, as well as a motto. The leader needs to define the following clearly: Vision, Mission, Objectives, Goals and the Motto.

"Without change there is no innovation, creativity or incentive for improvement. Those who initiate change will have a better opportunity to manage the change that is inevitable."

—William Pollard

Vision	Mission	Objectives and Goals	Motto
What is the overall goal? Where do you place yourself/your venture? What is the future you envision? *A vision never changes. It is the motivating statement.*	What processes need to be adopted and implemented to manifest the vision into reality? *The mission is the present. It is about the processes adopted. Its prime function is internal. If fulfilled, it can change.*	What are the goals and objectives that need to be achieved? *These include measurable and non-measurable objectives and goals. These also include every micro goal, such as the daily aims, as the leader believes that every drop fills the ocean.* *If objectives fail, the mission becomes redundant.*	What is the purpose statement of the vision and mission? *This is a powerful slogan, in the form of a sentence or phrase, stating the guiding principles of the leaders and their ventures.*

"Minds are like parachutes; they work best when open."
—Thomas Dewar, Distiller, Businessman

2. Ideal inspirational, innovative leaders have to CREATE TRUST AND FAITH before implementing any of their innovative ideas. New ideas are not always accepted

initially; acceptance requires immense confidence of those involved. An innovative idea tends to attract whispers of doubts initially. The leader needs to create trust and faith in the minds of all. Innovative leaders have to be risk-takers and must first prove themselves, so that the others are ready to take on the new mission. I am often inspired by a wise statement once made by one of my colleagues: "Praise people for innovative thinking, even when they present impractical ideas. By giving them a chance to pursue their crazy dreams, one may reach dead ends, but that itself will show the way forward."

One who has an appetite for taking risks definitely uses these three C's for reasoning—Collaboration, Creativity and Communication. For, they know that only working in collaboration and inspiring every individual to lead themselves can motivate creativity and open communication to solve problems, cross obstacles and achieve every mission.

3. Deadlines are a must. Therefore, EMPHASISING SPEED AND FOLLOW-UPS is a compulsion. Thinking of grand ideas and sitting on them is easier than thinking of innovative ideas and working hard towards achieving them. After strategising a plan and building trust, the action begins. To complete each and every mission in order to arrive at the goal, a timetable that lays out the deadlines is a must.

4. It is important for leaders to INSPIRE AND MOTIVATE themselves and those involved in their innovative

mission. There would be roadblocks, upheavals and obstacles that could create setbacks; however, a positive and wise approach would help take the mission forward. After all, ideal inspirational leaders, being intuitive, do listen to the wisdom of their inner voice to achieve all their aims and aspirations.

I have seen how passionately one of my students went about holding an important leadership role in the executive committee of the student-led body, even though not all of them were confident of his managing skills. I took the risk of giving him the role of Undersecretary General and sure enough, his passion led him to improve his skills and he is doing a fantastic job. A similar case is that of C Mary Barra, the chairman and CEO of General Motors. Her innovative success mantra has been to build allies, not enemies. Doing collaborative work and team-building exercises can only help in being innovative and successful.

When it comes to innovation, challenging the status quo is where it starts. If you want to please all, you will please none. The real challenge of leadership is not settling for mediocrity by pleasing all (recall the Aesop's fable, 'The Man, the Boy, and the Donkey'). The real challenge of leadership is changing before you have to. I have always innovated and fathomed the future exercise before any perceived onslaught of challenges.

It is important to refresh the mind, build on creative thinking and bring what is in thought to the surface where it is manifested to the current reality. Hence, these exercises need to be practised and perfected every day.

Encouraging innovation is the key to finding a better way to do things, or to help make people's life easier. There are many ways to stimulate creativity and though you may never know when or where you'll have an Aha moment, there are a few practices you can adopt to trigger the innovation process.

Take inspiration from real-life stories of people who have made a difference by their innovative thinking. The actions of great leaders who brought about change in the past or the bright minds of today who are charting the future can enthuse people to follow in their footsteps.

Collaborating with others is a wonderful way to promote innovation, as ideas can spring from various sources, and can be examined from different perspectives. Group members can contribute to building on an idea, all bringing their own expertise or experience to the table to refine and polish the solution till it shines.

Creating an environment that fuels ideation also helps. Getting out of a physical comfort zone, or making that zone more conducive to innovation, can motivate people to unleash their imagination.

Sometimes, even the pressure of a looming deadline can fire up the brain cells and, metaphorically, turn carbon into a diamond. And some people are known to thrive under pressure, and give their best when faced with a tight deadline.

Here are some exercises which you as a leader can try out in any group—corporate or community—to encourage innovation. These could help address a current problem faced by the group, or develop a strategy that would help that community in the future. It's important to promote creativity and collaboration in these exercises, as that brings out a one-of-a-kind, ideal solution to the challenge, or a unique way forward.

1. ADDRESS A SPECIFIC PROBLEM

Get various departments or groups together and mix up the participants. Look at various challenges that need to be addressed—conserving electricity, saving water, garbage disposal, doing a CSR activity or anything that's a pressing issue. Arrive at a consensus on one critical issue for which the groups can find a solution. Ask them to do some research on the issue, speak to different stakeholders and brainstorm to put together an interesting presentation—not necessarily in slide format—on their discoveries. Give a specific time in which they have to work and keep the deadline sacrosanct. Keeping one eye on the clock will force them to come up with brilliant solutions and a highly-creative presentation. Then, gather all the groups together and have a panel of seniors evaluate their conclusions. Finally, find a way to implement the best solutions.

2. CELEBRATE WORLD INNOVATION DAY

The United Nations has designated 21 April as World Creativity and Innovation Day. Celebrate this day by forming groups and get them to choose an innovation from any area—ancient or new—that has had a positive and lasting impact on people's lives. The topics could range from the mobile phone, or the first flying machine, or rainwater harvesting or even the sandwich. They need to bring its creation story to life through various media—art, craft, digital shows, staging plays, or whatever they choose. The presentation should be made as interactive and engaging as possible, leaving the audience inspired and encouraged to be innovative in every walk of life.

3. REDESIGN SPACES

Given the right environment, innovation grows and flourishes. And that means setting the right physical space for people to be at their creative best. Workplaces should be inspirational, as people spend a majority of their waking hours in them. While you could leave it to professional architects and interior designers, you could also let your people suggest how the working area can be made more ergonomic in design, in terms of improving efficiency and adding comfort. It could mean re-laying out the furniture, creating collaborative spaces with bean bags and rugs, even opening up the windows to take advantage of natural light. Take recommendations from your participants, run a poll among them to rank the most innovative ideas and then get to work, creating your inspirational work environment.

4. START A GARDEN

It's good to have green spaces around you, as plants have a calming and healing effect on our senses. It's not important to have a green thumb; you just need to have a basic love of nature. Allocate spaces for groups and get them to plant saplings of flowering plants or herbs. Tending to them every day also builds responsibility in your team members, who would be fascinated to see buds bloom and taste freshly plucked herbs. They could also take home the fruits of their efforts, when they grow plants like tomatoes, capsicum, lemon grass, curry leaves, carrots, among others.

5. OPEN MINDS OFFLINE

Innovators pick up ideas from their surroundings, sometimes by observing and getting involved in philanthropic community work. There are always new things to discover and opportunities to learn outside your working area, especially when you are seeing it happen up-close or are fully hands-on in getting it done. Organise a trip to an offsite location where the group can pick up a certain skill from the locals or participate in a special project. It could be working on a micro entrepreneurship's assembly line, or learning how to make handicrafts from a small-town artisan, or helping to bring a village's irrigation scheme to life. There are extraordinary experiences to be savoured on a bird-watching excursion or an educational nature trek. Getting out of the workspace's four walls can be a mind-broadening as well as heart-warming experience.

6. MAKE AN OFFER THEY CAN'T REFUSE

You can let inexperienced individuals have a foretaste of the real world and its diverse challenges by giving them the responsibility of running their own business. The important thing to learn is how to stand apart from others and offer a product or service that has the potential to attract customers in droves. This is where innovative thinking has a key role, and collaboration plays a significant supportive role. One person with a great concept can enlist others to bring the idea to life. Set up a weekend marketplace where your groups can sell their products or offer their services to locals. Here, exotic fusion foods and healthy desserts could be on offer, along with classes on making videos for social media or hip-hop dancing. The joy of earning your "First Rupee" through your own hard work can be incomparable.

7. SWITCH OFF FOR SOLUTIONS

There's no telling when an idea will strike, though it usually happens outside working hours. Give your people a specific time period during the day to indulge in an activity they love doing or one that would assist in their personal or professional development. When you provide team members this free time, they have the opportunity to give their ideas free rein. Organisations have seen marked improvements in productivity, with people taking on greater responsibilities and exploring innovative solutions to various challenges. Of course, this would need a certain amount of monitoring and mentoring on the part of the leaders, but in the long run, it would play a positive role in impacting business growth and success. Given their own space and time, when utilised wisely, can help people generate some valuable ideas.

These are just a few examples; you would probably have many ideas of your own to inspire innovation in your group. Start by picking one of the above activities, and explore what it might look like in your context. Think about how you structure your team members' time and create more flexibility. See how you can organise space, and create a more user-friendly design. And, perhaps, most importantly, think about how you organise learning, and cater to people with diverse inclinations, fluid and reflective of real-world pursuits.

Here are some methods to improve innovation, creativity and on-the-spot thinking. These methods can trigger new and expansive ideas:

NO IDEA IS A BAD IDEA

Set the ground rules first. Start with a clear brief for your team, giving them all they need to know about the challenge at hand. Provide a short background and the relevant information that would help them build a foundation for thinking. This is to ensure they are all on the same page with regard to the goal to be achieved. Take a few minutes to relax, calm down and get in the mood for ideating, and then kick off.

Every idea is a good idea in the initial stages. When you sit down with your team to brainstorm, encourage a free flow of ideas. Use a white board to write them down. Or hand over a set of Post-its to everyone, and have them post their ideas on a board.

At this stage, do not evaluate the ideas; just allow people to let their creativity run riot. Thinking wild has helped generate out-of-the-box solutions and create innovations that have changed the world. This is the time to think of new approaches to the challenge faced by the room, and these may seem absurd at first glance. Tap into personal experiences, or what's trending on social media, or what people were discussing on your workplace commute— these give you a diverse range of sources that can inspire a solution.

Dig deep to find the insight that lies at the core of the problem, for understanding the very heart of the issue can help trigger ways and means to solve it.

What the group throws up at this point may just be raw concepts that are not thought through, but it is important to acknowledge and respect the contributions, and keep egging the team on to push themselves.

It's good to put a time limit to this activity, say half an hour or one hour, as it gives people time to think and also makes them adhere to a deadline, else they might keep rambling on. The pressure of a deadline could also help them think harder to come up with ideas. To encourage your team to keep thinking creatively, conduct this session at least once a month.

BE CURIOUS

Truly creative people are curious about everything. They are fascinated by the most offbeat topics and delve into them to expand their knowledge base. They store all kinds of information in their brain, which they tap to make connections that never seemed possible.

You first need to stock resources in your brain. There are two good ways to do it, by reading a lot and accumulating experiences.

Read things that keep you up-to-date with the latest news as well as what's trending. Delve into subjects that pique your interest; topics at which you could even become a subject matter expert. This is an age of information overload, so you need to balance the two—items of passing fancy which keep you informed or even entertained, and tune you into pop culture; and subjects that beg you to explore them in depth.

Feeding your intellect is one side of the coin; the other is acting on it. You will remember a concept better when you've done it yourself—when you aren't "given a fish, but are taught how to fish". It could go from building your own little compost pit at home that teaches you about recycling, or learning to sketch that gives you a new perspective of design, or mastering digital resources that could help you on the job.

What's fascinating about these two activities is that you will often find yourself going down another road while exploring a subject. One topic leads to another organically, and you end up making diverse connections and exploring intriguing new worlds.

Keep moving on to new things. The more varied your experiences, as well as your reading, the larger the mother lode you have to tap when you need to come up with ideas.

LEARN FROM FAILURES

Rejection is one thing we fear most, especially when it comes to putting forth our ideas to others. "What will they think of me?" has kept more people quiet and more great ideas unexpressed than anything else. But you never know until you try. Speak up and you may just find that your idea is the best one, and what you have started could be helped along by a supportive group into a game-changer.

Ask for constructive criticism if rejected, as that will help you do better the next time. By yourself, break down what you did and look at how you can improve things. Look at the challenge from different perspectives and push yourself to stand out from the pack.

It's okay to fail, but you need to learn from your mistakes. Keep practising to be innovative with the tools given below and soon the process will come naturally to you.

Here are some tools to help you be more innovative, and develop your creativity.

GAMES AND EXERCISES: A good round of physical activity can get your brain cells humming. Having a vigorous workout in the fresh air or in a gym, followed by a winding-down time, can help you concentrate on learning or getting into a creative mood.

MULTIMEDIA TOOLS: Make use of music, videos, images, sketches, speeches and the like to help your team understand concepts and expand their imagination. These tools encourage them to focus and absorb information as it is delivered in an interesting manner. In this digital world, where we spend a lot of time looking at our screens, it's best to use multimedia formats to encourage your group's creativity.

IDEATE TOGETHER: Teams brainstorming together can come up with solutions ranging from the simple to the spectacular. The key is to be open to all kinds of ideas and encourage contributions from all participants, so that each one feels he/she is a part of the team. However, follow-up action is important, so that all your innovative thinking does not stay stuck on the shelf.

HOBBIES: Having an activity you are passionate about helps in a big way when you need to de-stress from routine work. Pick up your guitar or colouring pencils, spend some time talking to your plants, play a stimulating word game on your mobile, do a bit of embroidery—make time for a hobby that you can indulge in by yourself. With this time out, you'll feel rejuvenated and look at your work with new eyes and fresh perspectives, and find a different solution.

INSPIRATIONAL READING: Mark out a time in your day for reading things that can inspire you to innovate. Choose your books, articles, blogs or other material well, so that you spend your time profitably. Do your research and learn from the best minds in the field you are in, or from those who are simply great sources of inspiration.

THE RIGHT ATTITUDE: When you are passionate about what you do, you'll do your best work. You will seek ways to do things even better, as you'll be coming from a happy space, where your mind is not fettered by unwanted obstacles.

Learning sessions become more interesting when you introduce them as a story. If you are creative, even the most difficult situation can be related to interesting stories.

With even the Knowledge and Human Development Authority (KHDA) emphasising that schools take measures for improving the quality of teaching and learning, these innovative ideas are sure to make teaching methods more effective.

Innovation is often thought of as the result of rare genius. To create a new solution to an old problem that is both more efficient and practical than older methods seems like the kind of thing only the truly gifted can accomplish.

Here's a little secret: anyone can innovate. While there are those select textbook geniuses who work hard every single day to create industry-shaking innovations, many of the best ideas come from "regular" people who just thought: What can I do to make this process or idea better/easier/faster?

However, the bigger challenge is making sure these great ideas don't go unnoticed in the organisations that these everyday innovators work for.

The real question is, "how can you get the teams in your school/organisation to not only be more innovative, but to also feel more comfortable sharing their innovations for the benefit of the organisation as a whole?"

One solution is to use some special innovation activities to help your teams think outside the box and be more creative. Here are a few activities that can help teams be more innovative:

STAY HEALTHY: A sound body means a sound mind. Following a good fitness regime and eating well takes care of your body, which in turn, keeps your mind healthy too. A good night's rest is important, to relax and rejuvenate your body and keep you alert and charged up to take on the day's physical and mental challenges. Some form of daily exercise, a well-balanced diet, 10-15 minutes of meditation, and time away from electronic screens should be part of your everyday routine. When you are well-rested, your body and brain will be primed to get you performing creatively, and to the best of your ability.

GET A BRAIN WORKOUT: Exercise your brain cells by solving puzzles, riddles, cryptic crosswords and other brain teasers. There are several books, websites and apps that can keep you occupied for hours, but the important thing is to stimulate your mind and start thinking in different directions. Choose the type you like best, from trivia to word puzzles, logic or mathematical challenges, a rebus or Rubik's cube, a 1000-piece 3-D jigsaw or Sudoku, mazes or Mensa tests. This builds your brain muscles, which you can later flex when you need to come up with ingenious solutions.

EXPLORE NEW PLACES: Broaden your horizons by travelling and you broaden your mind at the same time. Visiting different places gives you a treasure chest of experiences, which can help you approach challenges from different angles. Taking a trip outstation, where work cannot distract you, is an opportunity to gain knowledge by sightseeing, to gain experiences that you never would have had otherwise, and to create delightful memories that you can carry with you for a lifetime. All of this adds to your reserves that can be tapped when you need to think innovatively.

Following these suggestions can get people equipped and excited to ride a new wave of creativity and innovation.

9

IDEALISM

"An idealist is one who, on noticing that a rose smells better than a cabbage, concluded that it makes a better soup"

— HL Mencken

The English word 'ideal' has roots in the Late Latin word, *ideālis*, meaning 'existing as an idea, or archetype'. The word 'idealist' is said to have been first found in the English language in 1701, in an essay by John Norris titled 'An Essay towards the Theory of the Ideal or Intelligible World'.

Presently, according to the Cambridge Dictionary, an idealist is defined as, 'someone who believes that very good things can be achieved, often when this does not seem likely to others'.

An ideal leader is one who values principles over practical behaviour. Such a leader strives to be a role model, making what most consider an unreal goal, a realised destination.

Great leaders are both idealistic and realistic. They have a grand vision and great goals. They seek to close the gap between what is and what can be, but they have no illusions that success is either certain or simple. The idealist leader is forward-thinking, and a personified combination of the following qualities:

PRACTICAL: Practical knowledge helps in solving problems by taking the knowledge that you already have and effectively using it in the real world. It helps you to be open to various situations, managing, thinking, finding flexible ways to approach situations, and knowing how to deal with others. Usually, people who are practical are called street-smart. However, I call them people with immense common sense. Accumulation of common sense makes a leader more and more practical. While getting new people to work for an organisation, it is always practical to recruit people with multidisciplinary degrees and years of experience than a highly qualified team with no experience. The institution stands to gain from employees with lived experience rather than those who only have bookish knowledge.

PRAGMATIC: Being pragmatic is nothing but a linear practical way of thinking and doing. Settling for something lesser or lower in position in a job can be a pragmatic approach. A pragmatic person then would make use of the situation, reap the harvest and climb faster.

POSITIVE: If one believes that every cloud has a silver lining, then one is said to be positive. As a leader, if one gets anxiety-prone and stressed at every little problem that comes by, then the spirit of being positive is killed.

PROCESS-BOUND: It's understood that all institutes need processes in order to avoid chaos and misadventures. The leader has to be part of the standard operating processes, and engaged in the code of conduct at work.

The idealist leader believes that striving for perfection makes the world a better place. Examples of idealist leaders are Mother Teresa, Mahatma Gandhi and Nelson Mandela. This is not to say that idealist leaders only achieve mammoth goals, as those mentioned. Every leader should be an idealist, no matter how large a mission they lead. Every industrialist who incorporates Corporate Social Responsibility (CSR) is an idealist. Every mother who teaches her child the values of humanity is an idealist. I feel, if every human being nurtures idealist thoughts and pursues such activities, we can actually save the world from the impending environmental doom.

One of the most important skills of successful idealist leaders is that they know how to grab opportunities, as they present themselves.

Here are examples of two stalwarts who withstood the sands of time, and improved what already existed, in a meaningful way:

1. Mary Kay Ash of Mary Kay Cosmetics, when denied a promotion, was not depressed. Instead, she spent

her savings of $5,000, and "turned it into one of the largest, most successful multi-level marketing companies, at a time when female CEOs were still extremely rare". Mary says that she saw obstacles as an "impetus to create something new". We all know how multi-level marketing companies also provide so many opportunities for others to earn, empowering them to live better lives.

2. Thomas Edison didn't see failure as a sign to stop, but stuck on to the dictum, "Try, try and try again till you succeed." No wonder the great bulb inventor and scientist affirmed, "I have not failed; I've just found 10,000 ways that won't work." And imagine how his light bulb lit up homes after sunset, brightening lives thereon!

The idealist leader has a vision, or possibly a few visions that permeate the workplace and are manifested in the actions, beliefs, values and goals. With each new day, the vision becomes more powerful and is shared continuously by all. The idealist leader works upon the vision set for the organisation, with motivation. Such a leader is an IDEAL example, who inspires many to set, implement and follow their personal ideals:

i) Influential: Using one's leadership to be an influencer, and becoming the change.

ii) Dedicated: Working towards one goal with total devotion and foresight.

iii) Enthusiastic: Deep affection for the purpose, hence intensely passionate.
iv) Assertive: Once the goal and the target are understood, one becomes even more assertive as one knows the outcome before it has been achieved.
v) Learner: This is an important quality that elaborates Edison's statement quoted about failure. Mastery of anything depends on the openness to learn continuously.

As a principal and leader in education, my world is challenging. I feel, being ideal every day inspires students to also aspire to nurture their personality, to be an ideal, for themselves, and their future.

When leading others, the idealist leader imbibes the following traits, which ensures that every individual not only contributes to the success of their venture, but that the idealists too are leading themselves and their teams with the same enthusiasm. The idealist leader aspires to inspire every individual to contribute to the mission and feel ownership towards the venture, and has the power of being responsible.

The idealist leader should focus on being more expressive, rather than on being impressive. This means understanding people and empowering them, and creating a lasting impression. They don't believe in creating false impressions of power and status, based on their materialistic buying power.

The late Dr LH Hiranandani was one such leader.

An idealist to the core, he had the rich experience of having faced all odds in life before becoming famous.

He toiled day and night for his patients and demanded the same from his junior doctors. He would not tolerate laziness, unpunctuality or indifference to patients.

He was a people's man—a man who responded with affection more than anyone can imagine. He always went out of his way to help even total strangers. Such was his magnanimity that it earned him a great place in society, nationally and internationally.

We have been told as children never to be vain. Aesop's tales spell morals through stories like the vain crow, the proud peacock, among others. Shakespeare has given five examples of kings like Julius Caesar whose pride was punctured. Chasing vanity only leads to a false sense of confidence. Napoleon Bonaparte himself was a famous narcissist. Notorious rulers in history like Commodus (Roman Emperor) was so infamous that he was absolutely despised by his people. A number of Russian czars can make it to the list of terrible, vain rulers; the worst among them was Ivan the Terrible. During his reign, Russia became a powerful country, but as is roughly put, Ivan's only legacy remains the moniker, Ivan the Terrible, which he earned from his dastardly acts.

Some are living legends. Others have left a legacy behind, decades after their death. Here, we need to remember Mahatma Gandhi and Nelson Mandela. What made Mahatma Gandhi universally accepted as an ideal leader were the tenets of ethics and morals, the clear vision of the progress of self and society. He donned several caps and that made him a Mahatma. We can speak volumes of his greatness, but even if half of his traits are imbibed and focused upon, an ideal leader can be born. "You must be the change that you wish to see in the world," he said. Gandhi, father of the nation and philosopher, was one of India's idealistic leaders. Gandhi admitted that he was a 'practical-idealist'—his methods of 'Ahimsa' and 'Satyagraha' were the means he chose to bring about change for a better social order. He was a master strategist who knew it would be impossible to defeat the British by force. So he chose non-violent non-cooperation as the way to achieve independence for his country, a road that no one else had taken. To make this happen, he knew he had to first unify his country—divided by caste, religion and language—under one banner in the fight for freedom.

He started at the grass-roots, experiencing the life of the poorest of the country at his ashram in Sabarmati. It was here that he slowly built up his following and then set off on his life's mission of 'Sarvodaya'—the welfare of all.

As a seeker of truth and justice, he did his best to uplift the poor and marginalised in Indian society. He was a true empath with a deep reverence for life, sharing at a very personal level his people's pains and struggles, their joys and simple pleasures too. According to Pandit Jawaharlal Nehru, there was no one who knew the pulse of the people better than Mahatma Gandhi.

Right from his younger days when supporting a cause, there was no difference in what Gandhi thought, said or did—his life was an open book and he believed that you should 'speak as you think and act as you speak'. This set him apart as a person with integrity, whom people could trust because his vision was as clear as his morals. He was focused on what he wanted to achieve for his country as well as the ways to reach those goals.

For him, the nation always came first, before his personal needs. Transparency, spirituality and simplicity were not mere words to him; they were at the core of his everyday life and dictated his actions. He had the courage to back his convictions and always stood steadfast to his principles.

What is his legacy? He set the foundation for resolving conflicts through dialogue and peaceful protest; he promoted service, love and reconciliation as the foundation stones for a better world. We can be inspired by his dream for a democratic, self-sustaining India where peace and justice prevail, for he showed us the way to achieve this by the very way he lived his life.

Imagine a person who has spent 27 years in prison split between Robin Island and Pollsmoor Prison and Victor Verster Prison. Instead of feeling bitter and pensive about youthful years being wasted in fun and games, he emerged stronger. Nelson Mandela was a leader who followed the dictum of:

i)   Listening to all
ii) Observing situations
iii) Learning when to lead

Recently, when I went to Jodhpur and rode a camel, I came to understand idealist leadership traits one can learn from this animal:

- Leaders, in order to be ideal, should be resourceful like the camel, keeping reserves to be made available as per the requirement.
- Leaders must brave all challenges, by designing themselves to face the odds and vagaries of nature and other circumstances. The sea can be choppy and the weather can be rough; yet the camel tolerates the heat.
- Idealist leaders, like the camel, must learn to see the distance, by creating a vision for themselves. Keeping your sights on the future and helping your team see the vision of your desired future will neither have you leap, nor rush, just like the camel. They stick to the vision and lead the caravan.
- Every idealist leader must realise that we exist to serve, and not wait to be served.

While we're still in the desert, let us take some important leadership lessons from the 1962 Oscar-winning film *Lawrence of Arabia*. The movie tells the story of TE Lawrence, a young lieutenant in the British Army, who almost single-handedly brought together a group of quarrelling Bedouin tribes to revolt against the Turks during World War I.

What did Lawrence have that made his efforts a success? First, he found a common platform that would bind all the tribes together. He showed them the big picture: that they could rebuild their Arab nation and make it a power to reckon with once again. He convinced them that only by working together—and not as individual tribes—could they make this dream happen. He boosted their pride in past glories, which only they could regain when they fought as one people.

Rallying people under one banner and giving them a goal in which they take pride and have a personal stake can accomplish your objective easily. To achieve great things, it takes a leader who is sensitive to the ethos of the group, who accepts the advantages of diversity and who perseveres to unite his people and earn their trust by his actions.

A common impression of idealists is that they usually have unrealistic ideas and live in a dream world. They are perennial optimists loaded with positivity and grand thoughts, and look at the world with rose-coloured glasses. This is because of their naturally naive outlook on life, which makes others envy or pity them, as they are rarely critical of anything. Idealists can tend to spend more time dreaming about a brighter future than doing anything to make it happen. They can spend hours devising ways in their minds to build a better mousetrap, without actually putting pen to paper to design it.

As a philosophy, idealism believes that ideas comprise the only true reality, which has nothing to do with physical objects. When you see the world, you are seeing things that your mind has created. The Greek philosopher Plato was one of the first to present a view of idealism, stating that the physical world is continuously changing, yet there exists a world of ideas that is constant and real, and we use our minds to construct things in the world before us. In idealism, human perceptions take precedence over the material world.

Idealistic leaders keep the big picture in mind when it comes to addressing any challenge. They are confident of reaching their goal, and are more optimistic about getting a positive outcome. Visionary and imaginative, they are driven by an entrepreneurial attitude and are quick to take advantage of new opportunities. They can move fast from task to task, and they want the rest of their team to keep pace with them, which often is not the reality. They are usually ready to take risks, for they have firm convictions about their ideas.

Practical thinking and working marks a pragmatic leader. They get into the nitty-gritty of the action plan, and decide how the task will be accomplished, allocating clear-cut roles to team members, along with processes and timelines. Their attention to detail can sometimes seem like an obstacle to getting work done, but they too look at the big picture and take all the necessary, practical steps to design the workflow and prepare for any problems that may arise on the way to achieving the goal. Pragmatic leaders can be more accommodating and open to suggestions to improve the working process.

I would like to explain which leadership style is better. Should you be a pragmatic, realistic leader or an idealistic, visionary leader?

Take time to examine yourself and see which style you need to work on for yourself—idealist or pragmatic? Also, pay careful attention to your team members and see which bucket they fall into. Both leadership styles are needed in order to achieve the goals you set for your team. Good leaders are the ones who can blend both, balancing an idealistic vision with pragmatic action, or vice versa.

This style of functioning can be carried forward to the team working under you. It's good to have a team well-balanced with idealists as well as pragmatic people. Get the best of both worlds when putting together a team to launch a new initiative or drive a project. As the team leader, you need to get the two styles to collaborate and work in harmony, as this will help you develop a star team.

It is important to train yourself to be a strong leader by diversifying your thought processes, especially since you will be dealing with both, idealists and pragmatic people in your team. Stoked with different ways of thinking in your mental arsenal, you have the potential to drive innovation and create the best possible outcomes together with your people.

So, while it's best to blend both styles to achieve success, you need to support this with the right experience and expertise that both you and your team can bring to the table. Remember, it's best to have a balance of both styles in order to think and act like winners.

Idealist leaders share the following core characteristics:

They are blessed with boundless energy and enthusiasm, which they attempt to infuse into everyone around them.

Always action-oriented, they believe in carrying people along in their journey to a grand goal, with everyone learning and growing in the process. Self-improvement is one thing that keeps driving them and they tend to be very optimistic about the future.

Their aim is to see that their people and their organisation thrive, succeed and go on to greater heights. In corporates, idealists focus not only on the financials of their organisation, but also pay attention to the consequences the company's actions have in terms of ethics, environmental considerations and impact on the communities in which they work.

Idealists are extremely creative and some of them keep an open mind to suggestions that can help improve the plan. They love brainstorming with bright minds. They value teamwork and encourage equality among the people they work with. They ensure everyone has a chance to voice their opinions, as they love to see the team members getting along with each other.

They are driven by their intuition and are guided by ideas—some of which may seem quite fanciful and unattainable. Idealists may not be able to prepare a precise road map as to how the goal should be achieved, but they do not compromise when it comes to getting the right thing done. They are charismatic; they have the right skills to influence and motivate people, and have remarkable communication abilities—they make you feel as excited as they are about surmounting the challenge that lies ahead.

They are determined and hard-working, and maintain a high level of energy till the very end of a task as they want to achieve the best possible outcomes. However, they expect the same dedication from their team members too, as they set high standards of excellence. They do not like it when the team is not performing to the expectations that they have set, and can be quite impatient and intolerant at times. However, they can be helpful and inspiring, guiding others to reach their potential.

Idealists have a kind streak, and can be warm, genuine and caring. They place great value on long-term, cordial relationships and can be die-hard romantics with big visions and aspirations. You'll find them to be highly ethical, with a strong set of values, and they avoid being false and hypocritical. They are very spiritual, seeking greater knowledge of their true self in order to improve their own lives. Pure idealists are rare, and only a few will be found at the top of the corporate ladder.

David Keirsey, an American psychologist and Professor Emeritus at California State University, has defined four types of idealist leaders on his website: Idealist Champions, Idealist Healers, Idealist Teachers and Idealist Counsellors.

IDEALIST CHAMPIONS: Champions love to try something new all the time, and need to have exciting things going on around them. They like to explore new concepts and seek patterns everywhere as they believe the whole world is interconnected. They are passionate about their goals and inspire others to follow them. Collaborating and networking with people thrills them and they have great interpersonal skills. Enthusiasm and authenticity mark out the Champions, and they seek this out in others too. They are non-conformist and radical, highly creative and exuberant in nature.

IDEALIST HEALERS: This type tends to be passionate about reconciling conflicts, and seek to heal themselves and the world around them. They believe in harmony and unity, demonstrating incredible compassion and sensitivity to the needs and feelings of others. They are loyal and expect loyalty from others too. Worthy causes inspire them and they can be exceptional sources of inspiration to those who face the same troubles they have been through, as they can connect with people on a very deep emotional plane. Their dreams are all about service and helping others, even at considerable sacrifice to themselves.

IDEALIST TEACHERS: These leaders seek to bring out the best in their team members, and use their innate intuition to understand and engage people. The most charismatic of all, Teachers are highly vocal, expressive and empathetic. They have vivid imaginations and it can sometimes seem that they are far removed from reality. Charming and warm, they are excellent at nurturing, mentoring and supporting those who need them. They wield considerable influence over people who follow them, and never hesitate to share their wisdom with the world. Integrity comes high on their list of traits and they live according to deep-rooted, authentic values.

IDEALIST COUNSELLORS: Perfectionists by nature, Counsellors make first-class mentors who guide people to reach their potential. They thrive best while interacting one-on-one in a nurturing, meaningful relationship, connecting with people in a sincere, insightful manner. They usually avoid conflict and strive for harmony and integration in the groups they work in. They are quiet and private, and have a small social circle which comprises close and longstanding friendships. They like to retreat from the world once in a while, in order to rejuvenate themselves with contemplative meditation.

As an idealist, I work through ideas and perceive through imagination.

10

INTELLIGENCE

"If you would take, you must first give; this is the beginning of Intelligence."

— Lao Tzu

The roots of the English word 'intelligence' are found in the word *intelligentia*, meaning 'understanding, knowledge, power of discerning: art, skill, taste'. Its stems can be found in the Old French (12th century) word *intelligence*, 'faculty of understanding, comprehension'. The late 14th century texts indicate the word 'intelligence' being used in the English language, and it was listed to connote, 'the highest faculty of the mind, capacity for comprehending general truths'.

The *Encyclopaedia Britannica* 2006 defines intelligence as "…ability to adapt effectively to the environment, either by making a change in oneself or by changing the environment or finding a new one … intelligence is not a single mental process, but rather a combination of many mental processes directed toward effective adaptation to the environment".

This definition of intelligence has helped me remind teachers to refrain from calling children intelligent, or unintelligent on the basis of their academic scores. Every individual is intelligent; it is a matter of enabling one at a young age to use their intelligence appropriately.

The famous American industrial and applied psychologist Walter V Bingham mentioned, "We shall use the term 'intelligence' to mean the ability of an organism to solve new problems."

Every day we face new challenges, obstacles, road blocks, problems, which we need to solve. There is no manual of life that mentions one common solution to every problem. Instead, we have to find a unique solution to every problem that seems common.

Intelligence is not limited to the race alone, but for that matter, every living organism. Look at how creepers grow towards sunlight, even in the darkest and densest of forests and jungles. Obviously, no academic records determine their potential of finding sunlight. They solve their problem intelligently, finding ways around trees of all shapes and sizes.

Wildlife spares no time crying over their challenges. Instead, they face every ravage of time caused by climate changes, human encroachments and natural calamities, intelligently. They adapt to change. Those that do not, go into extinction!

In addition to the above definitions, I would like to add that intelligence is also the ability to learn quickly from a situation and adapt to the changes; or rather, bring about the required changes to solve the issue at hand.

Before going further into explaining the role of intelligence in leadership, I would like to say that in spite of the other definitions, one cannot undermine the importance of academics. While I reaffirm that an individual should not be classified as intelligent or unintelligent on the basis of their academic grades, I do not undermine the importance of education. Education is what gives the mind the ability to not only use, but also develop, intelligence abilities. I refrain from using the term 'Intelligence Quotient', as it is a measure of intelligence that classifies how able or challenged a person is. I have come across so many differently-abled individuals—physical, or mental or emotional—who excel in their areas of expertise. They are leaders in their own right, who are able to solve problems within their realm.

Education lays the foundation and equips one with skills and abilities that are faculties of intelligence, which brings me to an interesting research I read regarding multiple types of intelligence. According to Dr Howard Gardner, there are eight different types of intelligence that measure the range of individual potential. These include:

1. Linguistic intelligence ("word smart")
2. Logical-mathematical intelligence ("number/reasoning smart")
3. Spatial intelligence ("picture smart")

4. Bodily-Kinaesthetic intelligence ("body smart")
5. Musical intelligence ("music smart")
6. Interpersonal intelligence ("people smart")
7. Intrapersonal intelligence ("self smart")
8. Naturalist intelligence ("nature smart")

Each has been explained below:

LINGUISTIC INTELLIGENCE ("WORD SMART")

This refers to the oral and written command over a language. People with this intelligence are adept at grammar and putting together their words to have an impact. Their use of the sounds, sentence structures and dynamics of a language enhance their leadership qualities in a significant way.

PEOPLE WHOSE WORDS CHANGED THE COURSE OF HISTORY

ADOLF HITLER: "I know that men are won over less by the written than by the spoken word, that every great movement on this earth owes its growth to great orators and not to great writers," wrote Hitler in his book *Mein Kampf.* A highly charismatic speaker, Hitler earned his following among the people of Germany through over 5,000 powerful speeches that united them to his cause. Like Churchill, he wrote his own speeches and practiced hard to perfect his special brand of speech-making. Animated, hypnotic, filled with over-the-top facial expressions and gestures, Hitler's speeches were mesmerising, and serve as brilliant examples of oratory in world history.

JOHN F KENNEDY: His speeches were dramatic in every aspect, be it in the evocative words he used, or his variations in pace and volume, or the pauses for effect. Kennedy used his body language in his debates, alternating between charming and forceful, determined and accessible.

He was adept at delivering singular, memorable messages, like "Ask not what your country can do for you, but what you can do for your country", and "Ich bin ein Berliner". He had that rare ability in speakers, to have a conversation with his audience. His speeches were drenched with passion and integrity, and that's what made him so loved by his people.

MALALA YOUSAFZAI: She has spoken at the United Nations, the Nobel Prize Awards, Harvard University and numerous other august gatherings. The experiences that this young lady has gone through make her a truly exceptional personality, courageous and confident to make a difference in the world today. Why do people hang on to her every word when she speaks? Well, she has a powerful message to deliver. Her mission is to ensure education for all girls of the world—and a bullet could not stop her. She speaks to her audience heart to heart, calling them directly to act upon her words and join her crusade. She is focused on her goals, and makes them crystal-clear in her speeches. Her words are laced with empathy and hope, and the determination to find solutions for a better future.

MARGARET THATCHER: The first female Prime Minister of the UK, Thatcher is highly placed among the greatest orators of all time. One of her most famous quotes, delivered at the Conservative Party Conference in 1980, was: "To those waiting with bated breath for that favourite media catchphrase, the U-turn, I have only one thing to say: You turn if you want to. The lady's not for turning." The 'Iron Lady' spoke with confidence and authenticity, in a strong, assertive tone. Advised to speak intimately and slowly in her public addresses, Thatcher used to stand close to the microphone and would have warm water with lemon and honey to lower her pitch.

OPRAH WINFREY: From 1986 to 2011, *The Oprah Winfrey Show* was the highest rated television show of its kind. Her speech at the Golden Globes in 2018, on accepting the Cecil B. DeMille Award for Lifetime Achievement, has gone down as one of the greatest speeches in history. Here are her secrets: She makes the very opening interesting—by telling a story. Her words are personal, genuine and straight from the heart, delivered with warmth and simplicity. She believes in repetition for effect, as in this example: "For too long, women have not been heard or believed if they dare speak the truth to the power of those men. But their time is up. Their time is up. Their time is up." Her messages are clear and heartfelt, and she ends her speeches on an impactful, memorable note.

WINSTON CHURCHILL: A little known fact is that Prime Minister Churchill won the Nobel Prize in Literature in 1953, partly for his brilliance at oratory. His rousing speeches and broadcasts during World War II were powerful inspiration for his people, raising morale and rallying them against the enemy. Churchill believed: "Of all the talents bestowed upon men, none is so precious as the gift of oratory. He who enjoys it wields a power more durable than that of a great king. He is an independent force in the world."

He wrote all his speeches himself, and he claimed that he spent an hour working on every minute of a speech he was to make. His genius with the written word, coupled with his authoritative delivery, has made his speeches occupy a special place in the history of the world. Paying tribute to his skills, US President John F Kennedy said, "In the dark days and darker nights when England stood alone—and most men save Englishmen despaired of England's life—he mobilised the English language and sent it into battle."

LOGICAL-MATHEMATICAL INTELLIGENCE ("NUMBER/REASONING SMART")

People gifted with this intelligence are excellent at combining reasoning and logic, and are called upon for their strategic thinking and problem-analysis skills. They focus on connecting the dots in numbers, patterns and relationships.

Renowned efficacious CEOs who have exemplary understanding of Logical-Mathematical Intelligence and can be called masters of the same include:

BILL GATES: A genius at coding, Gates was also highly-skilled at finding solutions to technical challenges. The man who dreamed of bringing personal computers to consumers' homes, and who gave Microsoft Windows to the world, was gifted with logical-mathematical intelligence, which helped him analyse problems and come up with path-breaking solutions based on data and hard facts. In his Harvard years, many of his professors were impressed with his sheer mathematical brilliance. The programs he invented are used on most of the world's computers today, but he still keeps pushing himself and his team to come up with new ideas and innovations in technology. Gates has acknowledged the link between professional success and intelligence, as he once said: "Microsoft must win the IQ war, or we won't have a future."

INDRA NOOYI: Her Bachelor's of Science degree in physics, chemistry and mathematics from Madras Christian College has stood her in good stead over the years, as she climbed the ladder to become the first female and foreign-born CEO of Pepsi. She is responsible for launching the Million Women Mentors initiative at PepsiCo, which aims to get more young women to pursue careers in science, technology, engineering and maths, with female mentors to guide them along the way.

JEFFREY R IMMELT: After studying applied mathematics at Dartmouth University, this CEO of General Electric did his MBA from Harvard Business School. He states: "I use my math major every day—I don't use the MBA quite as much." He feels that running his company is really about problem-solving, something he learned in his college days, due to "the inherent intellectual curiosity around math and physics".

REED HASTINGS: A math problem he had to solve in graduate school was the trigger for Hastings to set up Netflix, one of the most in-demand video streaming platforms in the world today. He had to work out the bandwidth of a station wagon carrying tapes across the US. Says Hastings: "From that original exercise, it made me think we can build Netflix first on DVD and then eventually the internet would catch up with the postal system and pass it."

SERGEY BRIN: The co-founder of Google studied at the University of Maryland where he did a double major in mathematics and computer science. His exceptional skills at mathematics proved invaluable in the early development of Google, a name inspired by the mathematical term "googol," which stands for the numeral 1 followed by 100 zeroes.

STEVE BALLMER: A whiz-kid who once beat Bill Gates in a math competition, this former CEO of Microsoft graduated from Harvard University with a degree in applied mathematics. It was said that he knew as much about the company's financials as the CFO at any time, and had a prodigious memory for all kinds of figures.

SPATIAL INTELLIGENCE ("PICTURE SMART")

It is all about recognising images and making connections to other objects surrounding them. The right side of the brain is utilised to understand 3-D images and shapes, and it is employed when you are solving puzzles, or playing games like chess, or map-reading, or designing a construction project.

Two famous people with spatial intelligence are Leonardo da Vinci—the renowned painter, engineer and architect; and IM Pei—the architect of legendary landmarks like the Louvre Pyramid (Paris), Suzhou Museum (China), Rock and Roll Hall of Fame (Cleveland) and Bank of China Tower (Hong Kong). They were gifted with the ability to see objects in their mind, manipulate and transform them, and then bring their visions to life in remarkable constructions.

The following artists and explorers are fine examples of people with spatial intelligence; more so, because they had a disability, but this never hindered them from using their skills to make a name for themselves.

ADMIRAL PEARY: American naval officer and explorer of the Arctic.

VINCENT VAN GOGH: The Dutch post-impressionist artist, famed for 'Sunflowers' and 'The Starry Night' paintings.

MARC CHAGALL: The French-Russian painter whose styles included Cubism, Expressionism and Surrealism.

HENRI DE TOULOUSE-LAUTREC: The French painter and lithographer, best known for 'At The Moulin Rouge' and 'Portrait of Vincent van Gogh'.

Other spatial-intelligent greats include MF Husain, Pablo Picasso, Neils Bohr, Galileo Galilei, Gustavo Eiffel, Frank Lloyd Wright, Andy Warhol, the Wright Brothers and Walt Disney.

BODILY-KINAESTHETIC INTELLIGENCE ("BODY SMART")

Leaders with this intelligence use their bodies effectively, as they are blessed with exceptional coordination and balance, perfect timing, clear body language, flexibility, speed and the talent to handle objects with dexterity.

LIONEL MESSI, SOCCER PLAYER: The star of FC Barcelona and Argentina's national soccer team is fascinating to watch for his coordinated body and footwork skills on the field. His control of the football is legendary; a talent that has won him six FIFA Player of the Year awards, six European Golden Shoes and the Laureus award for 'Best Sportsman of the Year' 2020, becoming the first football player to win this prize.

CRISTIANO RONALDO, SOCCER PLAYER: With his lightning-flash speed and amazing dribbling and passing skills, Ronaldo has notched up over 600 goals in his career till date. A mainstay of Juventus FC and captain of the Portugal football team, Ronaldo is a five-time FIFA Player of the Year awardee and has scored the highest number of goals in the UEFA Champions League.

NEYMAR, SOCCER PLAYER: His spell-binding footwork has mystified many an opponent, while his speed, passing and dexterity has made him a favourite with fans and team members alike. His on-field finesse earned him the all-time highest fee for a soccer transfer: 222 million Euros from Barcelona to Paris Saint-Germain in 2017.

OTHER NOTABLE BODY SMARTS: Canelo Alvarez, boxer; Roger Federer, tennis player; Russell Wilson, football player; Aaron Rodgers, football player; LeBron James, basketball player; Stephen Curry, basketball player and Kevin Durant, basketball player, to name a few.

MUSICAL INTELLIGENCE ("MUSIC SMART")

This comprises learners who enjoy using a musical multiple intelligence lens and demonstrate greater sensitivity to sounds, rhythms, tones and music. Since there is a strong auditory component to this multiple intelligence, they will often use songs or rhythms to learn and memorise information. You may find a child or colleague facing a challenge or who is weaker in one of the multiple intelligences. You can help them out by getting them to tap their stronger intelligences through specific activities that balance out their weaker areas.

AR RAHMAN: His love of experimentation sets Rahman apart in the world of music, a man described by *TIME* as the world's most prominent and prolific composer. With influences ranging from Carnatic, Hindustani and Western classical music to modern electronics and technology, Rahman turns out a unique blend of Eastern, Western and World music, which never fails to appeal to a universal audience.

He has won a slew of awards at home and abroad, including two Academy Awards, two Grammy Awards, a BAFTA Award and a Golden Globe. Acclaimed as the man who redefined contemporary Indian music, Rahman has contributed to the success of numerous films. Nicknamed "the Mozart of Madras", improvisation and orchestral themes are his signature, along with modern beats and sounds that make his compositions uniquely 'Rahman'.

ALEXANDRE DESPLAT: With a host of awards and nominations for his work, Desplat is one of the most popular and successful film score composers in the movie industry today. His portfolio includes *Harry Potter and the Deathly Hallows, Zero Dark Thirty, Argo, Godzilla (2014), The Shape of Water, The King's Speech, The Imitation Game* and *Little Women (2020)*. And this is in addition to a vast collection of soundtracks for other language films.

His versatility is his trademark, as he traverses genres and styles to make each of his scores unique. From science fiction to monster flicks, from high drama to fast-paced action, from children's movies to romantic tales, Desplat has done it all. Along the way, he has bagged two Academy Awards, three BAFTA Awards and two Golden Globe Awards.

ILAIYARAAJA: With over a thousand films and more than 8,000 recorded songs under his belt, Ilaiyaraaja is a true legend in the Indian music industry. To his credit, he was the first Asian to score a symphony for the London Philharmonic Orchestra.

Hailing from a family of musicians, he composes music that appeals to all ages, as well as the classes and the masses. His talent lies in his ability to evoke a spectrum of emotions with his tunes—ranging from joy to sadness, thrills to tenderness and rage to tranquillity. His songs are the backdrop for social celebrations and often convey hard-hitting political messages. Through his music, Ilaiyaraaja was instrumental in bringing attention to the plight of the working man and the rural poor, highlighting their struggles and dreams.

JOHN WILLIAMS: Who can ever forget the electrifying opening music of the *Star Wars* films? The grand orchestral masterpiece is the composition of John Williams, and is one of the many unforgettable scores he has written for movies like *E.T., Schindler's List, Jaws, Jurassic Park, Saving Private Ryan, Harry Potter, The Adventures of Tintin* and the *Indiana Jones* films.

His unique virtuosity can be seen in his wide-ranging repertoire, where the orchestration, melody and harmonies blend perfectly to match every mood and moment on the screen. He constantly reinvents himself, and he scores in old-fashioned style, without using technology.

With reference to John Williams being honoured with the American Film Institute's (AFI) Life Achievement Award, AFI President and CEO Bob Gazalle had this to say: "This man's gifts echo, quite literally, through all of us, around the world and across generations. There's not one person who hasn't heard this man's work, who hasn't felt alive because of it. That's the ultimate impact of an artist."

RAMIN DJAWADI: Some of the most popular film and series scores in recent times have been composed by this German-Iranian musical genius: *Game of Thrones, Prison*

Break, Iron Man, Pacific Rim, Clash of the Titans, Jack Ryan and *Westworld,* among others. Winner of Emmy awards and nominated for Grammy awards, Djawadi has over 100 soundtracks and film scores to his credit.

Mentored by the famous Hans Zimmer, the themes he composes range from orchestral to guitar rock to electronic and percussion-driven pieces. Djawadi states that his special blend of ethnic, Middle Eastern and Romantic influences earned him his spot for *Game of Thrones.*

INTERPERSONAL INTELLIGENCE ("PEOPLE SMART")

Sensitivity to others is at the heart of this intelligence. Those who are 'people smart' can interact very well with others, and are perceptive about others' feelings, moods and frames of mind. They are adept at reading voice modulations, body language and facial expressions. Here are some of the most well-known names in psychology today:

EDWARD F DIENER: With a PhD from the University of Washington, Diener is currently Professor Psychology at the University of Virginia and at the University of Utah, and a Senior Scientist with the Gallup Organization. His area of research is subjective well-being, which studies the level of happiness that people attribute to themselves. His findings state that people who say they are the happiest are those who have the strongest interpersonal ties and social support networks. According to him, extraverts are happier than introverts and people are more drawn to those who exhibit happiness. His work has also shown that subjective well-being has many positive benefits on one's health and lifespan.

Diener has published over 300 articles and book chapters, and has written a number of books like *Happiness: Unlocking the Mysteries of Psychological Wealth*, *The Science of Well-Being* and *Well-Being and Public Policy*. He is the recipient of many honours in his field, including the William James Lifetime Achievement Award for Basic Research from the Association for Psychological Science, the Distinguished Scientist Award from the American Psychological Association and the Distinguished Scientist Award from the International Society of Quality of Life Studies.

HOWARD GARDNER: A developmental psychologist, Gardner is currently the John H. and Elisabeth A. Hobbs Professor of Cognition and Education at the Harvard Graduate School of Education and Senior Director of Harvard Project Zero. His speciality is education and his theory of multiple intelligences is what he is best known for, which has been explained in brief in this book. Gardner has been actively involved in school reforms in the United States, and in projects that promote excellence, engagement and ethics in education. His goal is to help prepare students to become good citizens who make a concrete contribution to the well-being of society. His current research on a national scale among students, parents, faculty and education administrators aims to gather valuable suggestions on how to provide quality higher education in the future.

His most popular books include *Frames of Mind, The Shattered Mind, Multiple Intelligences: New Horizons and Five Minds for the Future.* Among numerous other awards, he has been honoured with a Lifetime Achievement Award from The Mensa Foundation, the Prince of Asturias Award for Social Sciences, and he was selected by the American Management Association as one of the Top 30 Leaders in Business.

MARIANNE SCHMID MAST: Currently Professor of Organizational Behaviour in the Faculty of Hautes Études Commerciales at the University of Lausanne, Switzerland, Mast's research deals with how individuals in hierarchies interact and communicate verbally and non-verbally with each other. Her work applies to all kinds of organisations, and she uses modern technology in her investigations. She set up her own immersive virtual reality laboratory at the University of Neuchâtel which she uses for studying social behaviour and conducting interpersonal skills training. Her studies have thrown new light on negative self-perceptions based on gender stereotypes that impact women in social interactions.

The books she has authored are *Gender Differences in Dominance Hierarchies, Gender and Emotion: An Interdisciplinary Perspective* and *The Social Psychology of Perceiving Others Accurately.*

PAUL EKMAN: The popular TV series *Lie To Me* is based on the work of Ekman, who has been called 'the human lie-detector'. Professor Emeritus of Psychology at University of California, Berkeley, he is widely recognised for his work on non-verbal human communication, which encompasses facial expressions, body movements and hand gestures. His 'atlas of emotions' has links to over 10,000 distinct facial expressions and his research on micro expressions has been helpful in various fields where screening techniques are required.

His published work spans a number of peer-reviewed journal articles and book chapters, and includes books like *Unmasking the Face; Telling Lies: Clues to Deceit in the Marketplace, Politics, and Marriage; Emotions Revealed: Understanding Faces and Feelings* and *Nonverbal Messages: Cracking the Code: My Life's Pursuit.*

STEPHEN D REICHER: Reicher studies group behaviour and relationships at an individual-social level. A Professor of Social Psychology at the University of St. Andrews, Fife, UK, he is an acclaimed authority on crowd psychology. He has been published extensively on topics like crowd action, leadership, nationalism, intergroup hatred and conformity. Currently busy constructing a model of crowd action that will drive social change, Reicher is also working on building social categories through language and action, and researching mass mobilisation around the issue of national identity.

He is a Fellow of the American Physical Society, a Fellow

of the British Academy, a Fellow of the Royal Society of Edinburgh, and is the recipient of the Harold Lasswell and Nevitt Sanford awards from the International Society for Political Psychology. He is co-author of the book *Self and Nation*.

VS RAMACHANDRAN: Richard Dawkins says this about him in an article which appeared in *The Guardian*: "Ramachandran is a latter-day Marco Polo, journeying the Silk Road of science to strange and exotic Cathays of the mind." It's a glowing tribute for Ramachandran's stellar work in the field. Currently, he is Director of the Center for Brain and Cognition and Distinguished Professor with the Psychology Department and Neurosciences Program at the University of California, San Diego, and Adjunct Professor of Biology at the Salk Institute, California. While he started off researching visual perception, it was his experiments in behavioural neurology that broke new ground in how we think about our brain.

His invention of the Mirror Box was revolutionary as it helped ease phantom limb pain, which is felt by people who have lost a limb. His key contributions to the field are in the space of mirror neurons, synesthesia, sleep paralysis and autism. Named one of the 100 most influential people by *TIME* in 2011, he has been honoured with the Padma Bhushan and was named 'Scientist of the Year' by the ARCS Foundation in 2014. He is the author of the best-seller *The Tell-Tale Brain*, as well as *The Emerging Mind* and *A Brief Tour of Human Consciousness: From Impostor Poodles to Purple Numbers*.

INTRAPERSONAL INTELLIGENCE ("SELF SMART")

Usually more at ease working on their own, these people are very self-aware and mindful of their own emotions, ideas and objectives in life. They are focused on their goals, and while they tend to look inward, they are also great empaths.

KYLIE JENNER – KYLIE COSMETICS: She started off selling her make-up on the Internet and in select small stores. In 2018, Kylie smartly signed an exclusive distribution deal with Ulta, a beauty retailer with an extensive presence across the USA. Her signature range of lip kits, coupled with a brilliant pricing strategy, enabled her brand to take on the bigger names in the cosmetics industry and get the cash registers ringing. With a billion-dollar beauty label and dozens of brand partnerships under her belt, Kylie Jenner is rapidly emerging as the most entrepreneurial member of the Kardashian-Jenner clan. Kylie Jenner might only be 22 years old, but the reality TV star presides over a business portfolio to rival American scions three times her age. At her formative age, Kylie has now become America's youngest ever self-made billionaire, overtaking Facebook's founder Mark Zuckerberg who hit the figure aged 23.

JEFF BEZOS – CEO AND FOUNDER, AMAZON: Starting up from his garage, his online bookstore grew into one of the most phenomenal success stories in the global business world. With his idea, he made the most of the untapped potential on the Internet and entrenched online shopping as an integral part of our everyday life. Diversity in its offerings is Amazon's hallmark and Bezos has ventured into numerous side businesses that are proving to be success stories in themselves.

Self-smart people are skilled at identifying their own strengths and weaknesses. They enjoy planning and setting goals, and often need time to be alone to process their experiences and/or for creative expression.

On 27 June 2008, Bill Gates stepped down from being the Chairman of Microsoft, the software behemoth he had built from scratch with Paul Allen. His new goal in life was to focus on altruistic causes like education, health, development and climate change, to help make the world a better place. The second-richest man in the world now devotes most of his time to the charitable foundation he set up—The Bill & Melinda Gates Foundation, and has donated billions of dollars to various causes over the years. Bill is in charge of setting the overall direction of the organisation, shaping the grant-making strategies and being a spokesperson for the Foundation's various projects.

Guided by their belief that 'every life has equal value', the couple travels across the country and all over the world to champion the causes that the Foundation is involved with. They have funded projects in 135 countries; in developing countries, they focus on improving health facilities and addressing hunger and poverty issues, while in the USA, they help people who do not have the resources get opportunities to build their lives and succeed at work and at school.

Some of the key partnerships of the Foundation include the GAVI Alliance, which works to bring vaccines to the world's poorest countries; Mama Cash—the longest-running international women's fund; the Dangote Foundation in Nigeria which is helping eliminate malnutrition in the country and The Gates Millennium Scholars Program which provides financial support to students of colour pursuing undergraduate degrees.

NATURALIST INTELLIGENCE ("NATURE SMART")

A deep love of nature is an outstanding quality of this set of people. They are highly-sensitive to the environment and are most at home in a natural setting. They love interacting with animals, and are skilled at growing and nurturing all kinds of flora and fauna.

ALYSSA ADLER: The great ocean deeps hold a magnetic fascination for Alyssa, who has ventured underwater with her video camera in some of the most off-the-beaten-track locations. Though she gets to capture the most amazing marine life on film, she also finds heaps of trash dumped on the ocean floors.

While she has travelled across the globe, she prefers exploring the extreme cold conditions of Antarctica and the Arctic. Through her films, she wants to show the world the beauty of the deep waters, and get people to understand the impact they have on polluting these pristine environments. She believes that it is important for young scientists and entrepreneurs to step up and employ their creative minds to make conservation a priority, not just an option.

GERALD DURRELL: Best known for the book *My Family and Other Animals* and a number of other entertaining stories, Durrell was a zookeeper, naturalist, conservationist, author and television presenter. He set up the Durrell Wildlife Conservation Trust to breed endangered species and educate people about them, as well as the Durrell Wildlife Park on the island of Jersey, where species of all kinds are preserved, especially those that are under the threat of extinction. His books are filled with hilarious and enjoyable tales of his real-life experiences with a variety of animals, and always display his care and sensitivity towards them.

Born in Jamshedpur, India, his family moved to the island of Corfu when he was young, and this was where he developed a lifelong love for all living things. He has travelled the world to study and pick up animals for his zoos. Desmond Morris, famed zoologist and author of *The Naked Ape,* said: "His most important contribution to zoology was in the field of animal conservation and what became known as Durrell's Army—the people he trained from around the world to go back to their own countries and save animals for themselves."

HANS COSMAS NGOTEYA: When you grow up, like Hans did, with the Serengeti plains all around and Kilimanjaro looming nearby, you cannot help but develop a deep love for nature. This young Tanzanian found his calling in environmental conservation, and soon helped set up the non-governmental organisation Landscape and Conservation Mentors in order to support and improve communities through sustainable environmental practices.

With a passion for filmmaking and photography, Hans is exploring practical solutions to conserve wildlife and encourage communities to co-exist with their natural surroundings.

MALAIKA VAZ: Her passion for the great outdoors has taken Malaika down various trails. A conservationist, wildlife filmmaker and *National Geographic* host, she has travelled across the globe in search of adventure. In addition, this 23-year-old has worked tirelessly for a variety of causes, such as empowering underprivileged youth through adventure sports and outdoor education, investigating the illegal trade pipeline in manta rays across Southeast Asia, and helping victims of sexual abuse.

In her series *Extinction*, she puts the spotlight on lesser-known species like the Red Panda, Great Indian Bustard and the Purple Frog, while also telling the stories of the scientists and communities fighting to ensure their survival. Her goal is to popularise conservation and get more and more young people to connect with nature.

MANEKA GANDHI: Her love for animal life led Maneka to set up People for Animals in 1992, which has evolved into the largest organisation for animal welfare in India. She was Chairwoman of the Committee for the Purpose of Control and Supervision of Experiments on Animals (CPCSEA) and has been instrumental in setting up a sterilisation programme for stray dogs, replacing the municipal method of killing them.

A patron of International Animal Rescue, Maneka has also brought to the forefront the issue of commercial exploitation of animals in her weekly television programme *Heads and Tails*. Her love for animals reflects in the books she has authored: *Animal Laws of India, There's a Monster under My Bed, Wise and Wonderful* and *Heads and Tails*.

MEDHA PATKAR: An activist who fights for people's rights, Medha is also an environmentalist who founded the Narmada Bachao Andolan to help conserve the environment and get justice for the people displaced from their homes by the project. Medha has been part of the World Commission on Dams, which has carried out comprehensive research on the environmental, social, political and economic impacts of the development of large dams globally and their alternatives.

Her simplicity and courage have gained her the love of tribals and marginalised people everywhere. According to Medha, the greatest challenge we face today is to tackle dwindling natural resources by encouraging alternative lifestyles, and this is where she devotes most of her energies.

As humans we have a great ability to learn and solve problems. We are innovative, creative and inventive, which all together makes us very intelligent. While we call ourselves intelligent leaders, there is no denying the fact, as mentioned previously, that animals exhibit signs of intelligence as well.

Chimpanzees are close to human beings and besides developing instincts of empathy, altruism and self-awareness, they perform much better than human beings on memory tests. If cats are adaptable, dogs perhaps could get the tag of being the most intelligent. It is the only intelligent animal that can read the mind of the master and behave accordingly. The crowning achievement of elephants is that they are great team players.

The above exemplified traits of animals are centred on the mind. All great leaders follow their mind first and then their heart. The heart nurtures feelings while the mind spells out clarity and caution. Intelligence is all about mind matters that help build emotional resilience. When asked by someone what intelligent leadership was, John Mattone, an authority on intelligent leadership and coach of Steve Jobs, had just one thing to say: "(Intelligent leadership is all about) a strong mature environment in the inner core, which increases the probability to execute great things in the outer core." In the case of all intelligent leaders, the heart and mind decide a perfect balance between the two, making one tackle challenges and solve problems. It helps in decision-making.

Intelligence has also been classified as the following types:

Listening intelligence: The ability to listen and communicate effectively.

Verbal Intelligence: The ability to express oneself with clarity.

Hobby Intelligence: The ability to pursue a hobby, or multiple hobbies.

Reasoning Intelligence: The ability to reason out, analyse and make decisions.

Besides the CAP—Creative Intelligence, Analytical Intelligence and Practical Intelligence—I feel we must also look at intelligence under the categories of social intelligence and emotional intelligence, which every leader must master.

Emotional intelligence is about the matters of the mind, while social intelligence implies the heart as the ruler. Emotional well-being means a positive sense of well-being that enables individuals to face challenges in day-to-day life. Developing emotional intelligence is highly recommended for developing an ability to perceive, examine and manage emotions of the self and others. As leaders, we need to connect our emotional intelligence to management styles.

One afternoon, a fortnight before the school annual day function, the headmaster called for a staff meeting after the students left. The teachers walked in slowly, some after the headmaster was already in the staffroom, while a few others made excuses and left for the day. The headmaster was appalled by the turnout. He was angry, yet maintaining composure, he said to the teachers present, "We are stewards of this school, and have a responsibility towards the growth of the institute. If you can't be here on time, you can't expect discipline in class, or results from the students." The next day, he sat with his deputies and they decided to chalk out strategies, goals and deadlines. The teachers implemented it all till the end of the term, and by the end of the year, academic as well as non-academic targets were met.

My research on emotional intelligence has brought out a few golden competences that help in building good emotional balance.

LOGICAL INTELLECT

Every problem has a solution. It is said the questions can be as important as the answers. In the recent general election when a major political party lost, emotions ran high and a blame game rent the air. On analysis by experts, the gaps were closed and the political party performed better. Every leader, be it a school leader or a corporate leader, must refuel upon the mistake committed and close the gaps.

ADAPTABILITY: When Nora changed her school and went to a bigger town from a smaller one, she just couldn't adjust in the new school. The teachers seemed like monsters and her friends were too difficult to deal with. The teachers found her to be an introvert and could only sermonise the parents to teach her adaptability and adjustment. However, on reflection, the head of the school took the child's case seriously, and took on the onus of teaching adaptability to the child. The teachers were asked to spend more time with her for the first week every day, and identify her talent. She was put in groups till she was identified as a wonderful singer and creative writer. Just as much as we teach adaptability, it is also on us to adapt to new individuals. A change in jobs, roles and projects should not hurt.

By being adaptable, one increases opportunities, improves relationships, and thinks clearly and constructively.

RESISTANCE: If one cannot develop resistance, one can never grow emotionally strong. Resistance teaches us how not to crumble or grumble. It teaches you to stand tall and weather the storm. Remember the childhood story of the hugging tree: "On a bleak and lonely rock, by a vast and mighty sea, grew a lonely little tree, where no tree should ever be." A tree grows precariously on a cliff side just because a little boy hugs it, as though whispering into its ears not to bend and break in spite of the heat, strong cold wind, or storm brought on by the vagaries of nature.

SOCIAL INTELLIGENCE: It is all about attitudes and behaviour in response to one's social environment. A leader is considered to be socially intelligent, as long as one has the skill to navigate social relations. Today, the world is ridden with numerous problems caused by a lack of peaceful co-existence, which is the outcome of leaders with poor social intelligence. Gone are the days when society was traditional, awareness was less and people were ignorant. The 21st century of Gen-2 and Gen-Alpha requires social enrichment, all the more because artificial intelligence has made the world a smaller place, where networking is concerned.

Every intelligent leader negotiates social relationships and accomplishes goals in the social environment. I do it with a lot of humour. As a school leader, 'Humour in Uniform' is a catchword for enhancing social intelligence for me. Here is a personal anecdote:

HUMOUR IN UNIFORM

Who has not heard of the play, 'Post Early for Christmas'? The parcel at the post office causes commotion and confusion all because it contained a tick-tick clock neatly packed and ready to be posted away to a distant land. The confusion and commotion did it. It became a hilarious story at the end of it all, as it was a bomb hoax.

If the Defence Forces use humour in uniform, then we in schools also have our share of humour in uniform.

School was about to close for the vacations. It was the last period and the school buses were lined up. Another hour and the dispersal of children would start. We have very cordial relations with our bus vendor, as we repose our faith in him to ferry our students back and forth from school and home. One such nice person is Mr Ashok, who prowls around like an owl disposing unwanted things and alerting the watchman of mysterious happenings around the school.

On one such day, Mr Ashok detected a strange contraption perched on a tree trunk 50 metres away from the school gate. It glistened in the sun. It looked like a tiffin box with wires around it and ticked away to glory as a timer was placed within the box. It definitely looked like an IED (Improvised Explosive Device). That very morning, Ashok read in the newspaper about bombs being hurled by youth and some planted on the roads in Kashmir. There were also homeless people roaming around the vicinity of our township searching for jobs. The scene and time for an untoward impending disaster seemed likely.

He informed the school and guards. All of us swung into action. The police were called in.

Whatever it was, we could not possibly take any chances. Time was literally ticking both ways for the supposed bomb to explode and the children to exit. The police were informed. The cop seemed more panic-stricken than us. He called the bomb disposal platoon to detonate the supposed bomb. In the meantime, some parents arrived to fetch their wards, while others, sensing trouble, streamed in to add to the confusion.

I called the Disaster Management Committee that I had formed in the school, formulated a plan and dispersed the children from the other three gates facing the school. The children thought a film shooting was going on, while we told them that the police were conducting their routine drills, lest the children stayed back to catch a glimpse of their favourite film star. Some smart alecs questioned, "Why the drill at this time?" I replied, "To test how we handle children during dangerous situations."

The area was cleared out and the bomb squad arrived

to deactivate the suspicious device at around 12.30 pm. A grumpy-looking, sleepy-headed young lady, aged about 25, came out of the gate adjoining the school and walked towards the contraption. She confessed, "This is my invention." She was a research student of the nearby prestigious institute. At the police station she revealed, "I had obtained permission from my institution to test the instrument which I developed. However, I failed to inform my institute, as well as the other institutions where I have placed the device on Monday. I apologise for the panic situation I have caused."

The bomb detection squad dismantled the device. The bomb scare was over. Fortunately, it was a hoax. We were relieved and the press hovering around kept asking for my comment. "All's well that ends well. Nothing can be taken lightly. Rather be a butt of laughter and ridicule, than be overtly smart and get caught in a disastrous situation," I said.

A headline in the next day's paper read, 'Weather Device Sparks Panic Outside a School'. Our comments were published as follows:

The Principal said, "One of our bus drivers saw the device placed outside our school and alerted us. Students leave through that gate so we had to be careful. We were not informed about the project in advance."

One Senior Inspector of the area said parents and school authorities panicked on spotting a device with wires. "The bomb squad carried out an over two-hour operation to dismantle the device. After cutting the wires, it was found to be a device developed by a research student of a prestigious institute to test temperature and humidity. The student said she placed 15 units across the area of the nearby school to check their functioning," he said.

We all laughed the next day, a laugh worth a million. Ashok was suitably rewarded. The cop was recognised for the effort and the student was asked to teach the older classes physics, and clear their doubts on weather and climate. However, she never came, and I still keep waiting for her.

What have we learnt?

Ready Wit, Presence of Mind, Practical Sense and Social Interaction always come to the aid of leadership.

You don't need qualifications in degrees to be intelligent. All intelligent leaders work through wisdom and experiential learning. A truly intelligent self never wallows in the self.

Meditate for minimum of 12 to 15 minutes at a time to get health benefits. That's not very long. In fact, the more research that is done on meditation, the more apparent it is that it's not about doing it for hours at a time—it's just about doing it regularly.

So, consider making meditation a practice. Give your brain a rest. It may just help you become even more of a genius. Meditation increases your intelligence and raises your IQ.

Meditation increases intelligence in many ways: From making both brain hemispheres work together, to boosting memory, to increasing brain size, to enhancing emotional intelligence (EQ).

Here are nine reasons why meditation creates the perfect environment for intellectual growth and learning:

1. MEDITATION ENHANCES YOUR BRAIN'S FORM AND FUNCTION: Science has proved that meditation increases the thickness of the cortex and boosts the grey matter density in your brain. Your neurons become more flexible and the connections between them can reach even further. It's like a gym workout that increases your physical muscles. This has numerous benefits, ranging from better sensory processing and cardio-respiratory control, to helping you reduce stress and increasing your ability to learn new things.

2. MEDITATION IMPROVES YOUR MEMORY: When you meditate, there is a significant increase in activity in two areas— the hippocampus and the frontal lobe. This enhances both long-term and short-term memory, which is necessary for all your everyday functions. When we meditate, our brain takes all the different, disorganised pieces of information and sorts them into neat slots, thus creating enough memory space.

3. MEDITATION IMPROVES YOUR ABILITY TO CONCENTRATE: With so many distractions in our lives today, it becomes hard to pay attention to any one thing. Meditation helps you calm down and gets your mind relaxed. It is like mental hygiene, as it removes clutter, adds clarity and fine-tunes your talents. With meditation, you can stay focused and sharp, able to concentrate on the job at hand.

4. MEDITATION STIMULATES CREATIVITY: Meditation puts you in a positive, peaceful frame of mind and this is most conducive to thinking creatively and being innovative. It helps you look at challenges from different angles and come up with original solutions. At the same time, it also opens you up to other people's suggestions and lets you see the good points in their ideas. Meditation can boost your self-confidence and courage to face any setbacks or negative feedback when putting forth your ideas.

5. MEDITATION BRINGS BALANCE TO YOUR LEFT AND RIGHT BRAIN: In our daily routine, most of us tend to use our left brain more, the hemisphere that deals with logic, maths and language, among other things. When the right brain is also brought into play, you will find it easier to solve problems, focus better on tasks, and be more insightful in your thinking.

6. MEDITATION MAKES YOU MORE INTUITIVE: Meditation connects the conscious and unconscious parts of your brain, linking your instinct with reason. With its soothing effect, meditation facilitates the bridging of the two and helps power your intuition— the inner voice or gut feelings that you rely on for guidance every day. Steve Jobs has said that his revolutionary ideas came from his gut feelings (intuition) above all else.

7. MEDITATION BOOSTS EMOTIONAL INTELLIGENCE (EQ): Spending time meditating gets you in touch with your physical self, as well as your innermost

feelings and emotions. This boosts your emotional intelligence, as you can control your responses to external stimuli. You will be able to pick up other people's emotions better and respond to them in the appropriate way.

8. MEDITATION HELPS YOU SOLVE PROBLEMS FASTER: You cannot find solutions when you are stressed and under pressure, as your hormones will start shutting down creative areas of your brain. Meditation relaxes you and creates the right environment to keep your creative juices flowing even when you are in a stressful situation.

9. MEDITATION MAKES YOU HAPPY: Spend time in deep meditation and you'll emerge in a much better mood. Detaching yourself from your problems for a while brings you enough joy to bounce back with a smile.

The below mentioned Neurobic Brain Exercises if practised every day will increase the brain capacity and make room for loads more information that can be stored in the brain.

DO YOUR MORNING ROUTINE DIFFERENTLY: Familiar kitchen aromas are probably what you wake up to every day. Try keeping another pleasant scent at your bedside table—peppermint or vanilla, for example—and inhale it when you first wake up. Retain the images and sensations that it conjures up.

Brush your teeth with the other hand, try a different channel for the morning news and use your non-dominant hand for the functions on your mobile phone. Initially, this can be a challenge, but you will slowly get used to it. Sitting in another place at the table, or having your breakfast in another spot can also open your mind to a different view.

BATHE WITH YOUR EYES CLOSED: Be careful when you're doing this and try not to hurt yourself. Remember where you've put things, and then feel your way about to get them.

TURN IT UPSIDE DOWN: Put things the wrong way up around the different rooms in your home. Your family photos, the wall calendar, artefacts or showpieces—of course, make sure they can't break in their new positions. Looking at these will force your brain to make a new connection.

CHANGE YOUR COMMUTE: Try another route. Whether you're walking your dog or travelling to work, go off the same old track. When travelling, if there's not too much pollution, leave your windows open. Keep not only your eyes, but ears and nose open for the new impressions you will pick up.

PLAY WITH COINS: Keep a few coins of different denominations in your pocket. While walking around, feel through them, handle them one by one and try to identify their value without looking at them. Stop on the side and check if you're right. This helps in improving your tactile senses.

PLAY 'SEVEN USES': Think of any everyday object and come up with seven different ways you can use it—real or imaginary—none of which are remotely related to its original use. A pencil could turn into a microphone, a baton, a telescope, a screwdriver, a fake moustache, a flagpole or a drum stick. This preps your brain for the times you need to come up with out-of-the-box ideas.

ACTIVATE ALL SENSES AT THE SAME TIME: Gardening and travelling are two activities you should try, as they get all your senses firing at around the same time. The sights, sounds, smells, the feel of different textures and the taste of new foods can open up your brain to gaining holistic new experiences.

PURSUE SOMETHING NEW: Sample a new cuisine, pick up another hobby. These new activities stimulate your brain as it comes to grips with something it has never done before.

DON'T RELY ON TECHNOLOGY: Keep your gadgets aside and try to do simple tasks that you usually use them for. Mathematical calculations, checking spellings, memorising a phone number, are some examples.

INTERACT WITH PEOPLE: Today, technology has eliminated many of our social interactions, but you can try and make some connections with people instead of bots during your day. For example, walk through the market or grocery store and haggle with the vendors instead of ordering online. This type of interaction helps improve your brain's cognitive functions.

CO-READ A BOOK: Take turns with a friend or family member at playing reader and listener. Each of you reads aloud different portions of the book. Your brain works differently when you are reading to yourself, as compared to reading out loud and listening to another person. You'll also find yourselves having a fun time together as you can try out different accents to tell the story.

Just remember, your brain will get used to the new activity over time—maybe days or weeks or even longer. And when it does, move on to another neurobic activity to give your brain a new workout.

> Human intelligence is the source of our problems. But it would be foolish to think that the solution is to reduce intelligence. There is only one way out: we must not let our intelligence be guided by negative and harmful emotions. It must be guided only by proper and positive motivation if it is to become marvellously constructive.
>
> —The Dalai Lama

11

INSPIRATION

"If your actions inspire to dream more, learn more, do more and become more, you are a leader."

— John Quincy Adams

Inspirare, meaning 'blow into, breathe upon', which figuratively means to, 'inspire, excite, inflame', is the Latin root word for 'inspiration'. Initially, in the 13th century, inspiration was defined as, 'immediate influence of God, or a god', which was actually a derivation from the Old French word *inspiracion*, meaning 'inhaling, breathing in'.

Initially, the adjective form of the word 'inspiration' was *inspiring* in the 1640s; and *inspirative* in 1770. The first use of the of the word 'inspirational' dates back to the 1800s, when it was defined as 'tending to inspire'.

The Macmillan Dictionary defines inspirational as someone or something, 'giving you enthusiasm to do, or create something'; 'extremely good, or skilful'; 'deserving praise, respect and admiration'.

To add to this, I feel being inspirational is being a role model who inspires others to lead their lives to greatness, through every setback, failure and obstacle. Success is the result one achieves on conquering every disadvantage one faces, and every weakness one replaces with strength.

There is absolute magic in every leader who can inspire future generations through action and deeds. In order to be an inspirational leader, one has to be impactful and impressive, albeit through openness about one's struggles, fears, weaknesses, failures, losses; all that one overcame on the road to achievement.

We all have role models. We have grown up admiring people. As a child at school, I always admired the Head Girl. Her mannerisms, way of speaking, and dressing up— all seemed fascinating. Every so often, I would find myself behaving like her, or rather copying the way she spoke, walked, approached friends and teachers, etc. I thought if I shadowed her, I would become like her and become a Head Girl too. My class teacher noticed this and once called me to the staff room, and sat me down to explain to me something important that remains with me to this day. She said to me, "Kalyani, it is good to have a role model who inspires you. However, do not try to imitate them to find your success. Individuality makes leaders, leaders. Monkeys mindlessly follow monkeys, thinking they are leading too. Being inspired means nurturing ambitions and wanting to achieve like the role model, but not imitating the role model. Recognise your own skills, and polish them into talents that lead you to being a leader. Greatness and success is not a comparison with another; but a comparison with where you were, and where you have arrived. It is constant, and continuous. If you aspire to be a Head Girl like her, then aspire in this academic year to achieve excellence as a human being first, apart from excelling in academics and other activities."

There are plenty of role models in every aspect of life. Good role models change your life forever, and help you discover your true self. This, in turn, helps to inspire others exactly the way you have been inspired. It was Robert K Merton who coined the phrase 'Role Model', alias Inspirational Leadership.

Why do we need inspirational leaders?

i) Inspiration creates a path for you to follow, emulate and reach your goal.
ii) Inspiration helps you identify your inner self, and enables you to become a better person.
iii) Inspiration aids you to be inspired always, and to inspire others always.

When I say "I lead by example," I mean I either set an example for others to emulate or I follow the example of my role model. Following is often followed by leading.

I always wanted to be a teacher, as I felt almost all my teachers had a profound impact on me; however, amongst my forever role models is my father. Almost every child claims, "My Daddy (or Mummy) is my superhero."

This is because we see how hard our parents work to not only keep themselves happy, but more so their entire family.

Abraham Lincoln is a fine example of an inspirational leader, who has taught us that failures are the pillars of success.

Lincoln, the sixteenth President of the United States who was aptly nicknamed 'Honest Abe', went down in history for his role in preserving the Union in the Civil War, and for the emancipation of slaves. His integrity and strong set of values made him an inspirational leader, as did his self-confidence and sense of responsibility for the decisions that he made. He had excellent communication skills, as was evident in his Gettysburg Address, and was a fine storyteller, who would captivate his audience and get them to share his vision. He could inspire trust, which he showed in a unique way, by forming a cabinet comprising all his political rivals. Lincoln was always open to discussion and debate, and acted on the opinions of others to correct his own mistakes. Humane in his dealings with people, he would go out of his way to help others and visited the battlefield and hospitals during the War to boost the morale of his soldiers. He made it a point to listen attentively to the different viewpoints of his cabinet members before taking a final decision. A time for relaxation and recuperation was high on Lincoln's list of priorities, for he knew the importance of getting rid of the day's stress, and he enjoyed spending time with friends and going to the theatre.

Og Mandino said, "Failure will never overtake me if my determination to succeed is strong enough." There are no secrets to success. It is the outcome of preparation, hard work, and learning from failure over time.

> Success is not final, failure is not fatal: it is the courage to continue that counts.
>
> —Abraham Lincoln

What should the youth imbibe and emulate from leaders?

My simple formula for being an inspirational leader is the sum total of every aspect of EMPATHY.

1. Encouraging and become more empathetic as well as understanding.
2. Moralistic, keeping ethics and values in the same sphere.
3. Persevering, the only key to success through hard work, dedication and devotion.
4. Attitude needs to be positive, assertive and confident.
5. Trustworthiness as well as honesty, truthfulness and loyalty go a long way.
6. Humanity, philanthropy, humaneness and being charitable are a must-travel terrain.
7. Yielding—It's the H_2O of life comprising humbleness, openness, accommodation.

Encouraging and become more empathetic as well as understanding: An inspirational leader always has a wide streak of empathy which is useful for putting oneself into another's shoes and seeing things from their perspective. These leaders are good at building trust and convincing people of their ideas, as they are inclusive and understanding. It is easy to develop empathy as it is a skill that can be learned with dedicated, sincere effort.

Here are the stories of some famous empaths:

AZIM PREMJI: With regard to empathy, Premji has said that its real test is "not with people like us but with people who are different than us". Considered to be one of India's most generous citizens, his Premji Foundation is one of the five largest endowments in the world. Set up to improve the quality of education in India, the Foundation trains over 1,000 teachers in more than 40 districts in six states so that they can provide better education to students in government schools. Premji believes that "all progress is meaningless if we are not able to reduce the burden of human misery, and live in harmony with nature". He was the first Indian to sign 'The Giving Pledge', which was set up by Warren Buffet and Bill Gates to get the world's richest people to share some of their wealth for charitable causes.

ELEANOR ROOSEVELT: First Lady Eleanor Roosevelt was known for her caring attitude and gentleness, and she was one of the key players in the American civil rights movement. She loved interacting with people and listening to them—she would glean all the facts about a specific problem and then put her mind to solving it. She has done stellar work to promote education and improve workers' conditions, and has been Chair of the UN Human Rights

Commission. She encouraged people to get to know their communities better and work together to find solutions to the problems they faced. In her autobiography she wrote: "My interest or sympathy or indignation is not aroused by an abstract cause but by the plight of a single person whom I have seen with my own eyes. Out of my response to an individual develops an awareness of a problem."

MOTHER TERESA: Leaving her Darjeeling convent in 1946, Mother Teresa followed her calling to live and work among India's poorest of the poor. She went out into the streets and welcomed the dying and destitute into her care, feeding them, looking after their health and well-being and helping them die with dignity. Mother Teresa's selfless service and kindness towards every suffering person, irrespective of their faith, have been an inspiration for many who have stepped out in service to carry on her good works all over the world. Her 'Missionaries of Charity' organisation touches both rich and poor in over 136 countries today, and she was honoured with a Nobel Prize as well as a Bharat Ratna. Her compassionate deeds also merited her canonisation as a saint by the Catholic Church. Her life's motto was: "Do small things with great love."

OPRAH WINFREY: One of the biggest successes in the entertainment world, Oprah came from a background of abuse and family problems and this built her determination to help others struggling to overcome adversity in their lives. She can connect at a deep, intimate level with guests as well as the audience on her show, actively listening and drawing them into her world, making them feel understood, appreciated and respected. She has the rare talent of making people feel connected, and has always maintained an open mind to diverse points of view. Oprah encourages people to be their best selves in order to achieve happiness and well-being. She has helped many through her charitable organisations; getting them access to education, mentoring people to become leaders in their communities and doing her bit to protect human rights. She believes that, "Where there is no struggle, there is no strength."

RATAN TATA: His deep-rooted value system and desire to uplift the underprivileged, inculcated by his grandmother, have carried him through life and he has always sought to impart these values to people he interacts with. During his early years working on the shop floor, he came up-close with the plight of less fortunate workers, and this was the trigger for him to do something to improve their lives. He brings the same business acumen as Chairman of the Tata Group to his philanthropy work, investing smartly to drive growth via innovative solutions. His ability to treat all people equally and his empathy for all classes lie behind his dream to see India as an equal opportunity country, where anyone can succeed as long as they have the willingness and endurance to go the distance. His vision is, in his words, "...to do something in nutrition for children in India, and pregnant mothers. Because that would change the mental and physical health of our population in years to come."

Other than being empathetic, keeping ethics and values in the same sphere is also important.

Persevering through tough times is the only key to success through hard work, dedication and devotion.

> A dream does not become reality through magic, it takes sweat, determination and hard work.
>
> —Colin Powell

People can never achieve success if they only daydream about it. To achieve your dream means to envision it first, and then through your actions, efforts and hard work, achieve a desired result and goal.

All of us have big dreams or ambitions about our lives. We all want to be successful. We want to achieve something big and great. To achieve success, we need to work hard and pay attention to our work and job. Success is present in each and every act, whether it is small or big. Whatever work we do, we need to put our heart, mind and soul into even our smallest acts with full dedication; only then will it result in success and achievement. Instead of sitting and dreaming about success, getting down and starting to work on it with pure devotion, dedication and determination will lead us to success.

You should be positive, assertive and confident: With these three qualities, you can be firm about the things you want, without stepping on the toes of others. Your self-assurance is balanced with empathy, as you consider the needs and viewpoints of others, while putting your own across in a reasonable manner.

Being positive, assertive, confident is usually viewed as a healthier communication style. Being assertive offers many benefits. It helps you keep people from walking all over you. It can also help you from steamrolling others.

Confidence, maintaining a positive attitude and being assertive can help you in many different ways:

- You have a better self-image, with a greater sense of self-worth
- You become more effective and productive
- You can follow a balanced lifestyle, and stay in control of your everyday routine
- You act and speak with conviction and assertive body language
- You can manage and mentor colleagues and juniors empathetically
- You can handle stress easily and are emotionally relaxed
- You are better organised and have more time and energy for things that matter

"Simple honesty of purpose in a man goes a long way in life," said the author Samuel Smiles. Besides, honesty strengthens bonds and creates more meaningful relationships. The foundation stones for balanced success are honesty, character, integrity, faith, love and loyalty, according to Zig Ziglar. Trustworthiness as well as honesty, truthfulness and loyalty go a long way.

Humanity, philanthropy, humaneness and being charitable are a must-travel terrain. As Carlos Wallace has said, "It's difficult to be honest with others when you continue lying to yourself."

Philanthropy is more than just giving money to a worthy cause. It should come out of a heartfelt desire to better others' lives and encourage them to stand on their own feet. There are many people of affluence and large organisations who assist charitable projects on a major scale, providing monetary support and getting their employees to volunteer their time.

Yielding: It is an essential life skill comprising humbleness, openness and accomodation.

In his Ted Talk, 'Be Humble — and Other Lessons from the Philosophy of Water', Raymond Tang explains the three lessons he learned:

"Water's humility taught me a few important things. It taught me that instead of acting like I know what I'm doing or that I have all the answers, it's perfectly okay to say, 'I don't know. I want to learn more, and I need your help.' It also taught me that instead of promoting my glory and success, it is so much more satisfying to promote the success and glory of others. It taught me that instead of doing things so that I can get ahead, it is so much more fulfilling and meaningful to help other people overcome their challenges so that they can succeed. With a humble mindset, I was able to form a lot richer connections with the people around me simply shifting my focus from trying to achieve more success to trying to achieve more harmony, I was immediately able to feel calm and focused again. I started asking questions like: Will this action bring me greater harmony and more harmony to my environment?

I became more comfortable simply being who I am, rather than who I'm supposed to be or expected to be. Work actually became easier because I stopped focusing on the things I cannot control and only on the things that I can."

You would have come across many leaders who are known for these virtues. What did you observe about them that caused you to form your opinions? They must have demonstrated these characteristics in tangible ways, and your experiences would have led you to say that they are reliable, honourable and worthy of respect.

Transparency is one important characteristic of great leaders. They say exactly what is on their minds, even when it is awkward, but their aim in doing so is to give constructive criticism. By being honest with you, they want to help you grow and improve. You know you can count on them because they stick to their promises and always come through for you.

Integrity in an office environment is established when a person follows the right work ethic, delivering on tasks as promised, as per the directions given or demonstrating proper workplace behaviour. It is also staying true to your values and having the courage to stand up for them even when they are at odds with your seniors' point of view or against a general opinion.

Trust is built when people are confident of your abilities because you have proved it to them time and again. When you put the needs of others or your organisation's requirements ahead of your own and fulfil them first, you earn a reputation for trustworthiness. Standing up for colleagues, supporting them when they need it most and maintaining confidences go a long way in building trust at your workplace.

As Raymond Tang has said, "Without force or conflict, I believe we can find a greater sense of fulfilment in our endeavours by shifting focus from achieving more success to achieving more harmony.

We also live in a world today of constant change. We can no longer expect to work to a static job description or follow a single career path. We too are constantly expected to reinvent and refresh our skills to stay relevant. In our organisation, we host a lot of hackathons, where small groups of individuals come together to solve a business problem in a compressed time frame. And what's interesting to me is that the teams that usually win are not the ones with the most experienced team members, but the ones with members who are open to learn, who are open to unlearn, and who are open to helping each other navigate through the changing circumstances. Life is like a hackathon in some ways. It's calling to each and every one of us to step up, to open up, and cause a ripple effect."

Whether you are a monk or not, young or old, leader or follower, lucky or unlucky, applying the three principles of humility, harmony and openness will definitely improve your life and the lives of those around you.

A perfect example of being an inspirational leader is the sum total of every aspect of EMPATHY. The Bill &

Melinda Gates Foundation is the perfect example that can explain how great leaders who have used all the above skills to become successful have built this space.

The Bill & Melinda Gates Foundation (BMGF), previously the William H. Gates Foundation, is the largest American transparently-operated private foundation in the world, founded by Bill and Melinda Gates. Based in Seattle, Washington, it was launched in 2000 and holds $50.7 billion in assets.

Charitable organisations are essential partners of the government in meeting social and economic goals.

At a global level, the Foundation focuses on healthcare projects and makes efforts to alleviate the poverty crisis. In the USA, they provide people educational opportunities and work towards making information technology easily available. The three trustees of the Foundation are Bill and Melinda Gates, and Warren Buffett.

POWER

Everybody would like to step into the shoes of anybody holding a powerful position or anybody commanding maximum respect. Nobody wants to be inspired by Hitler. Though he was powerful he was not well-respected. All would love to be like the Missile Man, Dr APJ Kalam, the erstwhile President of India. Parliamentarians too are indeed powerful and influential, but by being in contact with them, do I get the power? It is influence coupled with a road map charted towards a successful life that makes everyone follow such leaders. In the present world, there are countries with people whose strengths are limitless. They know how to push the boundaries on what we think is impossible. Had our scientists like Dr Homi Bhabha or Dr Kalam not shared their vision with everyone and guided their juniors with the right perspective, ISRO would not have earned worldwide respect; especially, Chandrayan-2 would not have been envisaged nor would the scientific research on cosmic rays in physics. It was Dr Bhabha's motivation that resulted in the development of an NMR spectrometer for solid state studies. Truly, it was with Dr Bhabha's powerful leadership that Tata Institute of Fundamental Research (TIFR) has become the cradle of India's nuclear research; truly inspirational.

PASSION

What does the word 'passion' mean? It is defined as any powerful or compelling emotion. To be inspirational, all leaders should exemplify passion at work, which means the leadership strategy is positive and full of passion, which inspires others to join and identify with your view.

All passionate leaders engage people to work harder, to go faster and to improve results.

Mother Teresa and Henry Ford's works can be truly inspiring as they were passionate leaders who were quiet, yet deep down they had a great sense of abiding commitment to a cause with a clear view and goal.

Mother Teresa spent 50 years working among the poorest of the poor in Kolkata and founded the order of The Missionaries of Charity. Her mission rested upon the words: "Give wholeheartedly to the poor." The same goes for Henry Ford. He kept going on despite business failure, till he could produce the Model T, his dream car that was not only reasonably priced, but reliable and efficient. I often tell my colleagues that what makes one truly successful is passion. The moment you start thinking of the benefits to accrue before your task is completed or while the task is on, your focus will be lost.

Lives of great men and women have taught us that to be truly inspirational, one has to be passionate—your love for your work will resonate with your team and passion becomes contagious. How true is this proverb: "Our passions are the winds that propel our vessel. Our reason is the pilot that steers her. Without the wind, a vessel would not move and without a pilot, she would be lost."

Inspirational leadership follows the dictum set by Denis Waitley: 'Chase your passion not your pension.' Passionate leaders inspire others to work, are vocal and excited about their work, and see to it that the employees too are passionate about their work.

A strong bonding exists between passion and inspiration.

PLAY

Great leaders inspire through play. They inspire through action. We live in deeds, not in years.

Ancient Indian teacher, philosopher, economist, jurist and royal advisor Chanakya said, "A man is great by deeds, not by birth." When we look around, we will see many beautiful things that inspire us. I like the way poet and dramatist Ben Johnson epitomised the attributes of an inspirational leader by describing the simple, sweet smelling lily as "A Lily of a day / Is fairer far in May / Although it fall and die that night— / It was the plant and flower of Light / In small proportions we just beauties see; / And in short measures life may perfect be."

Age does not define how inspirational a leader is. In fact, as long as the leader nurtures the traits of empathy mindfully, then even a class monitor can be an inspirational leader for his/her batchmates.

Anne Frank (German-born Dutch-Jewish diarist) was only 15 years old when she was executed. She had written a diary about what her life was like, while hiding from the Gestapo in occupied Netherlands. Her book, *The Diary of Anne Frank*, has inspired many youngsters to express their thoughts through various media.

Young sports champion Sania Mirza has inspired the next generation to pursue sports beyond just cricket. The movie *The Sky is Pink* is inspired by a young girl who had a degenerative autoimmune disease and became a motivational speaker before dying young.

> I attribute my success to this—I never gave or took any excuse.
>
> How very little can be done under the spirit of fear. Were there none who were discontented with what they have, the world would never reach anything better.
>
> —Florence Nightingale

FLORENCE NIGHTINGALE: England in the Victorian era generally regarded nursing as a lowly task, not one for genteel ladies. Naturally, it came as a shock to her family when Florence told them that this was the vocation she had chosen for her life, and they forbade her from pursuing the profession.

However, she believed that she had a divine calling to become a nurse, which stirred in her a strong desire to be of service to others. She diligently educated herself on the subject of nursing and in 1853, she took on the position of superintendent at the Institute for the Care of Sick Gentlewomen in Harley Street, London.

In 1854, reports of the Crimean War came in, describing the horrifying conditions for the wounded. Florence was authorised by her friend Sidney Herbert, the Secretary of War at the time, to lead a team of volunteer nurses to tend to the injured soldiers.

The conditions there were appalling, with poor hygiene, a shortage of medicines, overcrowding and mass infections. Florence appealed to the British government to improve the facilities and they sent in the Sanitary Commission to clean up and improve the living conditions.

She earned her nickname 'The Lady with the Lamp' as she would make her rounds of the patients alone when everyone else had gone to bed, bringing care and solace to the suffering.

Florence Nightingale was responsible for introducing proper training for nursing staff, and several of her students went on to become matrons at leading hospitals throughout England. She also did trailblazing work in the area of hospital planning, which soon spread throughout the world.

The Florence Nightingale Museum, which sits at the site of the original Nightingale Training School for Nurses, houses more than 2,000 artefacts commemorating the life and career of the 'Angel of the Crimea'. To this day, Florence Nightingale is broadly acknowledged and revered as the pioneer of modern nursing.

HELEN KELLER: This renowned author and philanthropist was only 19 months old when she contracted an illness in which she lost both, her sight and her hearing. Her tutor Anne Sullivan patiently taught her words—Helen learned the word 'water' when Anne held her hand under a running tap and spelled the word on her other hand. Once she made the connections, Helen was so excited that she made Anne teach her 30 new words that day itself. She was a gifted child and by the age of 10, she had learned Braille and the manual alphabet and could also use a typewriter.

She pushed herself and by age 16, she went to Radcliffe College and became the first deaf-blind person to earn a Bachelor of Arts degree.

When she was 22, Helen published her first book, *The Story of My Life,* which tells of her early life and determination to win over tremendous odds. She continued to write on a variety of topics; her books include *The World I Live In, The Song of the Stone Wall, Out of the Dark, Midstream—My Later Life, Teacher, Anne Sullivan Macy* and *The Open Door.*

In 1913, she went on lecture tours around the world, mainly on behalf of the American Foundation for the Blind. Owing to her efforts, many initiatives were taken in the United States, from building rehabilitation centres for the visually-impaired to making education available for them.

Like her books, her visits to various countries have inspired thousands of people around the world. She has brought hope to blind people everywhere and as Senator Lister Hill of Alabama said in his eulogy to her, "She will live on, one of the few, the immortal names not born to die. Her spirit will endure as long as man can read and stories can be told of the woman who showed the world there are no boundaries to courage and faith."

I find myself lucky that I have been given all the senses and they are all functional; however, these great people have inspired me to always go beyond myself to achieve my highest potential.

If these famous people with disabilities share something, besides their professional success, it is their ability for self-improvement. The lives of most of them have not been easy and precisely because of that, they are an example and inspiration.

ANDREA BOCELLI: Watching him sing in an empty Milan cathedral in his solo Easter concert during the COVID-19 pandemic was one of the most ethereal moments of all time. Childhood glaucoma and an accident during a football game left him blind at a young age, but his never-say-die spirit led him to pursue music and lend his voice to some of the most beautiful melodies ever created. With over 80 million records sold, Bocelli is one of the world's favourite singers and an inspiration to many for not letting his disability stand in his way. One of his most famous songs is 'The Prayer' which he recorded with Celine Dion, who had this to say about him: "If God could sing, He would sound a lot like Andrea Bocelli."

ARUNIMA SINHA: A brave Arunima tried to resist a chain-snatching attempt while travelling on the Padmawati Express in 2011. The hooligans threw her off the moving train and after the horrific incident, she had to have her left leg amputated. This loss did not deter her; this former national level volleyball player and football player fought all odds to achieve the unthinkable. Wearing a prosthetic leg, she became the first amputee to conquer Mount Everest, on 21 May 2013. There have always been new heights to conquer for her, and she is also the first female amputee to scale Mount Kilimanjaro, Mount Kosciusko (Australia), Mount Aconcagua (South America) and Mount Vinson in Antarctica, among others. Today, this Padma Shri awardee is a motivational speaker, who has penned a book *Born Again on the Mountain*, and runs a not-for-profit school for underprivileged, handicapped children.

FRIDA KAHLO: Afflicted by polio since her childhood, Mexican painter Frida Kahlo had dysmetria in her right leg as well as spinal trouble. At age 18, she met with a horrific accident that left her bedridden and in intense pain throughout her life. Overcoming this, she became a world-famous artist, her style instantly recognisable, ranging from Surrealist to Mexican folk art. She gained international recognition for her works like '*Self-Portrait with Thorn Necklace and Hummingbird*', '*The Two Fridas*', '*Self Portrait with Cropped Hair*', '*The Broken Column*' and '*Without Hope*'.

NICK VUJICIC: Being born with no limbs can be devastating, but Nick battled bullying, self-esteem issues, suicidal tendencies and depression to rise above and make a name for himself as a motivational speaker, author and inspiration for people across the globe. Through the non-profit organisation he founded—Life Without Limbs—Nick goes around the world bringing hope to people and showing them the beauty of life. With supportive parents and friends, he has overcome his physical challenges and loves painting, swimming, skydiving and surfing. He believes that, "We need to come together in love. It doesn't matter how you look. I don't care how ugly you think you are. You are beautiful just the way that you are."

STEPHEN HAWKING: Admired by millions the world over for his books *A Brief History of Time, The Grand Design* and *Black Holes and Baby Universes,* Stephen Hawking overcame his Amyotrophic lateral sclerosis (ALS) disorder to become one of the most eminent theoretical physicists in history. When told he had two years to live, Hawkins went to work with renewed energy, coming up with major breakthroughs in his field, and he lived to the age of 76. It's amazing how a wheelchair-bound man who could communicate only through cheek muscle twitches and a speech synthesizer could give spellbinding lectures and propound game-changing theories. His stellar body of work earned him 12 honorary degrees and the prestigious Lucasian Professorship of Mathematics at Cambridge, a position once held by Isaac Newton. Hawking once said: "It would not be much of a universe if it wasn't home to the people you love."

These are some of the best-known personalities at the international level and with the most famous histories of improvement, but every day, there are many similar stories surrounding us that we do not know about.

Inspirational is the final 'I' trait of leadership; and it is a summing up of every trait dealt with in this book. The purpose of this book is to help readers develop each quality that leads them to the ultimate goal of being inspirational. Therefore, this chapter has a lot of examples that are explained on the basis of all other 'I' traits that combine to make them inspirational.

The exercises and activities below help people become inspirational and recognise their ability to be inspirational as they will achieve their set goals.

1. LOVE WHAT YOU DO, DO WHAT YOU LOVE: You know where your passion lies, so pursue an activity that you will enjoy doing, every day. This brings meaning and purpose to your life, and you will excel at what you do. Those who watch you will be inspired by your way of working, and will try to emulate you

as they see you put your heart into your professional work, or your hobby.

2. TELL THE WORLD: You don't light a candle and then keep it hidden—you place it high up where it can bring light all around. Let those around you know when you are all excited by what you are doing. Enthusiasm can be infectious; it evokes curiosity and draws others to see and learn more about what gets you energised.

3. SHOW YOU CARE: People remember how you made them feel more than anything else. Listen carefully when someone is speaking to you—your buzzing phone can always wait. Make the effort to express gratitude and acknowledge someone else's achievement from your heart. Pay a genuine compliment to those who look like they need a boost that day. Being there for friends or colleagues and easing their pain even a little elevates you in their eyes. Be encouraging, show others possibilities they had never thought of and help raise their self-esteem when they fail—everyone needs a second chance to change and improve themselves. You earn respect when you put others' needs ahead of your own.

4. SHARE YOUR SUCCESSES AND FAILURES: People appreciate a streak of vulnerability; you cannot be perfect all the time. Your successes will inspire them, as will the times you fell short—if you are humble about it and show how you learned from your mistakes. This way, others see you as one of them, who experiences the same challenges as they do.

5. STAY CALM AND COLLECTED: People always notice how you react in a troubling situation. Raising your voice, losing control, finding fault with others do not show you in a good light. Remain peaceful at all times, as one slip can damage the good reputation you have worked hard to build. Thinking calmly and acting decisively cements the good impression others have of you.

6. OPTIMISE THE OPTIMISM: When you are capable of focusing on the positive all the time, you uplift those around you too. Life is full of ups and downs, but it always helps to take things in your stride and balance the good with the not-so-good.

7. DISPLAY INTEGRITY: People admire those who keep their word and are honest when they are not up to performing a task. Being dependable is one of the key traits of a leader; people know whether they can rely on you because of your past actions. Having a strong value system and living by it is also important.

8. BE CLEAR WHEN COMMUNICATING: Transparency and clarity are appreciated by others, so you need to make sure you communicate in a lucid, unambiguous style to ensure you are understood. This applies to both—what you say and what you write. When speaking to others, be articulate and maintain eye contact, as this helps you hold their attention.

Must-watch movies that will inspire you to never give up:

- *The Shawshank Redemption* (1994)
- *Rocky* (1976)
- *127 Hours* (2010)
- *Into The Wild* (2007)
- *Schindler's List* (1993)
- *It's A Wonderful Life* (1946)
- *Freedom Writers* (2007)
- *Amelie* (2001)
- *The World's Fastest Indian* (2005)
- *Forrest Gump* (1994)
- *The Pursuit of Happyness* (2006)
- *A Beautiful Mind* (2001)
- *Life of Pi* (2012)
- *The Pianist* (2002)
- *Rush* (2013)
- *Life is Beautiful* (1997)
- *12 Angry Men* (1957)
- *The Greatest Game Ever Played* (2005)
- *The Blind Side* (2009)
- *The Aviator* (2005)

"It is better to lead from behind and to put others in front, especially when you celebrate victory when nice things occur. You take the front line when there is danger. Then people will appreciate your leadership."

—Nelson Mandela

12

INTEGRITY

"Integrity is the ability to stand by an idea."

— Ayn Rand

The roots of the English word 'integrity' can be found in the Latin word *integritatem*, meaning 'soundness, wholeness, completeness'. It then found its way into the Old French word *integrité*, which means 'innocence, blamelessness; chastity, purity'.

Looking up the dictionary for the present day connotation of integrity, I found it to be a combination of the following definitions: 'adherence to moral and ethical principles; soundness of moral character; honesty; the state of being whole, entire, or undiminished; a sound, unimpaired, or perfect condition'.

In fact, integrity is one of my favourite traits of personality, and all the more of leadership. It is this quality of being honest and having strong moral principles that makes an individual a complete leader—a personality of utmost respect.

Maintaining integrity is one of greatest challenges for people in power.

As mentioned, the word 'integrity' comes from the Latin word *integritatem* meaning 'wholeness and soundness'. All leaders who are sound in character and mind are dependable, trustworthy and most reliable.

Stand up for what you believe, and you will always have the courage to take big risks. Every organisation is based on certain principles and policies, upon which pillars of greatness are built.

As a leader, you represent your integrity and gather respect from one and all. In fact, integrity is the wholesomeness that comes from self-respect. Leaders who own their soul with pride, their ethics with honour and their morals with clarity, always remain a driving force of inspiration.

There is no denying the fact that it is a privilege to work with leaders who are honourable, as they are the type of leaders who treat all ethically and respectfully.

In our climate change leaders of tomorrow, the young ones especially are true examples of holding onto their integrity.

'VIDYARTHI DEVO BHAVA': This slogan means that the student is god. 'Yuva Devo bhava, Yuva Shakti devo bhava'. Roughly translated, this means the youth represent the god of strength. As said by the Indian Prime Minister, Narendra Modi, the youth have the ability and the opportunity to change the world. From being job creators as entrepreneurs to their tech ability, the PM has emphasised the important role the youth of India has to play for the growth of our country and its economy.

Around the world, young people are mobilising by the hundreds of thousands to demand greater action on climate change. Driven by the understanding that the action that leaders take—or do not take—in the next decade will determine life and livelihoods for generations to come, these young people are striking from school and taking to the streets for a transformational change for people, the planet and our shared prosperity.

Here are some of the world's young climate activists (leaders) who have dared and defined their life for their nation.

GRETA THUNBERG: According to a study by UK media regulator Ofcom conducted in 2018 among 3,500 British students and parents, it was found that more children were likely to support social causes on social media, and 10% of 12-to 15-year-olds had signed a social media petition during the year. They dubbed this 'the Greta Effect'—inspired by Greta Thunberg, the teenage Swedish environmental activist.

In August 2018, she sat in front of the Swedish Parliament every Friday, holding a sign that said: "School Strike for Climate." Her goal was to get the government to address the carbon emissions problem, and she urged students across the world to join her. In a short time, her campaign went viral on social media and on 20 September 2019, 4 million people joined the global climate strike—the largest climate demonstration in history. Her #FridaysForFuture has snowballed across continents and Greta has travelled far and wide to address world leaders and get them to do something concrete for climate change. Named *TIME* Magazine's Person of the Year 2019, Greta has gained the support of activists, scientists and even the Pope.

In her words: "When haters go after your looks and differences, it means they have nowhere left to go. And then you know you're winning! I have Aspergers and that means I'm sometimes a bit different from the norm. And—given the right circumstances—being different is a superpower."

JOHN PAUL JOSE: This young climate activist is one of India's leaders in the #FridaysForFuture campaign. What triggered him into action was a statement made by UN climate change experts, that we had 12 years to save the planet. Seeing the apathy of local governments to do anything about the environment, Jose became very active on social media where he drives awareness about the problem and mobilises youth activists across India. Spreading international news about the climate issue and organising initiatives for action, Jose also shares photographs of India as a vast, beautiful place under the direct threat of climate change. He says: "We are the last generation that can do something. We can no longer pretend nothing is happening."

LEAH NAMUGERWA: One of Uganda's chief faces in the Fridays for Future campaign, she has come a long way in her fight against the climate crisis—from the picketing frontlines in her native land to meeting Uganda's Speaker of Parliament, to attending conferences in Rwanda, Kenya and Switzerland. At age 13, Namugerwa had seen her friends losing parents, schools and crops to mudslides and flooding, and this provoked her to act. She tweets regularly, pushing for existing legislation on climate issues to be enforced, and actively organises tree-planting and beach clean-up events.

"I want to raise a generation that cares about the environment," says Namugerwa. "At least if the leaders can't make a difference, we can make a difference. We, as kids, we're not too young to make a positive difference."

LUISA NEUBAUER: In Germany, the Fridays for Future campaign is in the able hands of Luisa. Just like Greta Thunberg, she too has rallied thousands of people of all ages to demand the government and corporates to take action about climate change. She has had plenty of experience in her journey to promote climate activism, having worked with organisations like 350.org, Young Friends of the Earth, Foundation for the Rights of Future Generations, Fossil Free Germany, and the German Green Party's youth wing. In school, she campaigned against plastic waste and fracking and in her college, she played a part in getting the administration to divest from its holdings in gas, coal and oil.

Luisa says: "We're bringing the topic of climate change to the dinner tables and the classrooms and the town halls. This is certainly a success in itself."

XIYE BASTIDA: Brought up to believe that "if you take care of the Earth, it will take care of you," Xiye is one of the young, powerful figures against the climate 'crisis' as she calls it. When her home town in Mexico suffered from drought followed by floods, she knew that something was upsetting the balance of nature, and even after her family relocated to New York City, she felt she had to do something about it. Inspired by Greta Thunberg, Xiye is a leader of the Fridays for Future climate strike campaign in her area. She brings deep commitment and passion to her activism and has organised numerous programmes to motivate youth to the cause. Xiye is part of the Peoples Climate Movement, as well as the Sunrise Movement and Extinction Rebellion. In 2018, she was honoured with the 'Spirit of the UN' award.

Regarding climate activism, she had once said: "It's too important. In 10 years I'm going to be 27 and I want to be worrying about my career or how many children I'll have—not worrying about where I'm going to live and whether I'll be living in a place that will be flooded, or flattened by a hurricane."

The combination of an independent will and a strong

character brings about integrity in human beings. When I think about integrity as a vital ingredient of leadership, I am reminded of the story of 'The Emperor's Seeds'.

The Emperor wanted to find the truest upon his counsel of ministers to advise him. To do so, he handed pots with seeds to a few of his ministers and asked them to return in a year, with a pot of seeds sown.

When they returned, each had stories and pots filled with plants. There was only one amongst them who stood quietly and held an empty pot. He confessed to the king that he had no extraordinary experience to share, no plant in his pot.

The Emperor announced him the leader of his ministry; as he was the only one who did not do anything to create a false impression. The seeds given by the Emperor were boiled and therefore, could not have grown into plants.

This is the power of integrity!

The quality of being true to oneself and having strong moral principles is what makes one pass the test of integrity.

When speaking of leadership and integrity, one movie that comes to my mind, which clearly exemplifies the fact that leadership rests strongly on the value of integrity is *Scent of a Woman*. Al Pacino, the famous Hollywood actor, as the blind Lt. Col. Slade, when speaking in defence of a boy called Charlie who is being punished, states the following:

"As I came in here, I heard those words, 'cradle of leadership'. Well, when the bough breaks, the cradle will fall. And it has fallen here. It has fallen. Makers of men, creators of leaders. Be careful what kind of leaders you're producing here. I don't know if Charlie's silence here today is right or wrong. I'm not a judge or jury, but I can tell you this: He won't sell anybody out to buy his future! And that, my friends, is called integrity. That's called courage. Now that's the stuff leaders should be made of. Now I have come to the crossroads in my life. I always knew what the right path was. Without exception, I knew. But I never took it. You know why? It was too damn hard. Now here's Charlie. He's come to the crossroads. He has chosen a path. It's the right path. It's a path made of principle that leads to character."

Leaders should lead by example. If the leader is weak, the integrity in the institution, society or at home will crumble.

How does one strengthen character leading to integrity? Essentially, one needs to have the courage of conviction. You don't act one way in one situation, and in another in a different situation.

> "We will never be able to tackle climate change without bringing climate into our culture."
> —Indian Prime Minister, Narendra Modi

A BRIDGE that is strong and has no vents or lines of crack is said to have integrity.

- **B** Boldness to stand by one's convictions.
- **R** Responsibility towards the self and others.
- **I** Individuality to stand up for oneself.

- **D** Dependability that allows others to build trust.
- **G** Goodness of spirit to recognise ethics and virtues that serve the betterment of society.
- **E** Ethical soundness that does not give in to greed and selfishness.

To be considered as a person of integrity, one needs to:

1. Exercise self-control.
2. Practise accountability.
3. Learn to survive a storm.
4. Live with people who live with integrity.
5. Be emphatic, empathetic and flexible to honest work.

1. EXERCISING SELF-CONTROL: It requires an indomitable spirit. Self-control comes with discipline. A good work ethic brings about self-control and very often, we find people being driven by herd mentality without any self-realisation. Also, it's important not to yield to obligation in cash or kind, even if it is for the organisation, as it can be viewed wrongly and the leader's image gets tainted in the name of integrity.

2. PRACTISE ACCOUNTABILITY: The leader is the captain of the ship. A fine tale of accountability and responsibility is the tale of INS Khukri and its brave captain, Mahendra Nath Mulla. The captain realised the ship could not be saved and gave the command to abandon the ship. He perished. There was no panic, no confusion; only evacuation orders were being given.

Whatever may be the case, the laurels can be shared

by all, but the accountability for any mishap lies with the leaders. These days, delegation is considered constructed as empowerment, but accountability is the final responsibility lying on the shoulders of the leader.

Here are some easy ways you can start to make yourself accountable:

WRITE THINGS DOWN: Make lists or notes in a journal or on Post-Its, or on your mobile phone—there are a number of apps that can help you do this. Some of the popular ones include EverNote, Trello, Todoist, MyLifeOrganized and TickTick. They help you focus on your tasks as per their priority and help your day get better organised.

WRITE A PERSONAL MISSION STATEMENT: Keep it simple and SMART: Specific, Measurable, Achievable, Realistic and Timely. Incorporate your values into this statement and work with it in mind every day.

CREATE MICRO-GOALS: Set smaller goals as they are easier to target and accomplish. Be committed to completing them as they help you achieve the bigger goal more efficiently. Go step by step in order of priority and you'll succeed faster.

REWARD YOURSELF FOR SUCCESSES: You work hard to achieve your goals, so when you do, give yourself not only a pat on the back, but a tangible gift as well. Some item that you crave, or a weekend break, or anything that makes you happy and recharges you for the next goal.

REVIEW YOUR WORK: Do this at regular intervals—monthly, quarterly, every six months or annually. You need to be brutally honest in this review, as this can show you the areas that need improvement and at the same time, help you enhance what you are good at. Look at only yourself in this process and do not seek to blame others.

GET FEEDBACK FROM OTHERS: Encourage your team to give you unbiased feedback on your good and not-so-good points. Of course, you need to earn their trust first, with no fear of consequences. This gives you a picture of the other side: how your people view you and where you need to improve in your interactions with them.

USE YOUR TIME WELL: See how you can maximise your productivity at work, and make the best use of your time away from office. You have only a limited number of hours in each day, so make sure you fill them with something valuable and worthwhile.

3.   LEARN TO SURVIVE A STORM: No two days of my life have been alike. Every day unfolds something new. Just as much as there are sunny days, so also there are cloudy days. Each day of my life is like a new page of a large book on an adventure. This is perhaps the case with all leaders. If everything would be smooth sailing, how can the ship and its captain feel the pinch of choppy waves and then realise the value of success later? A good leader faces challenges bravely. Challenges are a part of everyday life.

Andreas Nikolaus Lauda, famously known as Niki

Lauda, Austrian Formula One driver, said, "There will come some phases in your life when you think this is the end of your life and career but at that phase, you have to keep faith in yourself and get resurrected."

His story is one of guts and glory, of an incredible comeback after great hardships. In 1974, as part of the Scuderia Ferrari team, he notched up his first F1 victory and in the following year, he won five races, to bag his first world championship. In 1976, Lauda, concerned about the safety of the track at the Nürburgring in Germany, tried to get the other drivers to boycott the race, but to no avail. During the second lap, he lost control and crashed into an embankment. In this terrible accident, Lauda sustained severe burns, internal injuries and lapsed into a coma. Written off by most, he made a miraculous recovery and returned to racing just a few weeks later.

Overcoming all challenges, he went on to win his second championship a year later, as well as the 1984 title. Lauda and Britain's James Hunt had a legendary rivalry in the F1, which was brought to life in the film *Rush* in 2013.

Niki Lauda has the unique distinction of being the only driver in the sport of F1 to have been champion for both Ferrari and McLaren. He never let his physical disabilities from the accident get in his way; and went on to be a successful entrepreneur and consultant. He set up three of his own airlines—Lauda Air, Niki and Laudamotion; was an advisor of the Ferrari F1 team and a manager of the Jaguar team, and provided insights and commentary on

F1 for a German TV channel. He was inducted into the International Motorsports Hall of Fame in 1993.

4. LIVE WITH PEOPLE WHO LIVE WITH INTEGRITY: It is rightly said you are known by the kind of company you keep. In today's competitive world, very few people are able to present their true selves, but one can identify negative people and fair-weather companions. It's best to keep them at a distance and keep the company of honest and open-minded people. This helps in building a profile of integrity, and surrounding yourself with honourable people helps you to live with integrity too.

SIR LI KA-SHING: Working 16 hours a day in a plastics company was how Li started, having had to drop out of school to support his family, due to his father's death. The skills he acquired here helped him to set up his own company, selling high quality plastic flowers to the world.

From these humble beginnings, his hard work paid off and he soon built a vast business empire. Today, through his conglomerate company Cheung Kong Holdings, he has interests in transportation, real estate, financial services, retail, and energy and utilities.

What are the secrets of his success?

A voracious reader, he is self-taught in most subjects. Studying business and trade publications and learning from them gave him the idea for his first business, which he built and expanded through diligent efforts and dedication. Staying true to his values earned him a reputation for integrity and simplicity. He has given billions of dollars to philanthropic causes and is regarded as one of the most generous people around today.

Nicknamed 'Superman Li' in Hong Kong because of his business successes, Li was named 'Asia's Most Powerful Man' by *Asiaweek* in 2001. He has also been honoured as a Knight Commander of the Order of the British Empire, and was presented the first ever Malcolm S. Forbes Lifetime Achievement Award by *Forbes* Magazine in 2006.

As Li says: "If you don't have a big heart, you will not succeed."

5.   **BE EMPHATIC, SHOW EMPATHY AND BE FLEXIBLE TO HONEST WORK:** To be a leader of integrity, one has to be assertive not aggressive, one has to have empathy not sympathy, and finally, one has to avoid rigidity and be more flexible to ideas-leading work.

DHIRUBHAI AMBANI

You could say that this is India's most famous rags-to-riches story. The saga of Dhirubhai Ambani is truly inspirational, as his business success became the success of his countrymen, and his legacy stays strong in the hearts of people till today.

Selling bhajias at village fairs was his first business venture as a schoolboy; this was his way of helping his family make ends meet. The next port of call in his business journey was Yemen, where he went in search of opportunity and found work as a gas station attendant. When his company became a distributor for Shell products, he was promoted and got his first taste of the opportunities available in the petrochemicals industry.

In 1958, he returned to India and soon got into the textiles business. He launched the brand 'Vimal'—a range of polyester materials for saris and suits, and with smart marketing strategies, he made it a household name among Indians. Dhirubhai smartly wooed investors to his company Reliance Industries, and by the mid-1980s, they were having Annual General Meetings in stadia—so vast was the crowd of shareholders.

Dhirubhai soon expanded the Reliance business and it spread out to form giant organisations in petrochemicals, plastics, communications, IT, power, finance and textiles.

Intelligent risk-taking, the agility to capitalise on opportunities and grand dreams characterised Dhirubhai Ambani. He was honoured with the Padma Vibhushan, voted the 'Man of the 20th Century' by the Federation of Indian Chambers of Commerce and Industry (FICCI) and named the 'Greatest Creator of Wealth in the Centuries' by *The Times of India*. He was awarded the 'Dean's Medal' by Wharton School and received the *Economic Times* Lifetime Achievement Award.

His inspiring message is: "Think big, think fast, think ahead. Ideas are no one's monopoly."

These leaders are some of the most renowned people who inspire not only your mind for a time, but also impact your inner soul. When you read inspirational stories, you'll begin to see a few common threads and relate to them better. Integrity, hard work, passion, determination, and drive are all common elements of these stories. Surprisingly, obstacles, failure and incredible odds are also elements of these stories. They all will strike a chord, and I guarantee you they will inspire and encourage you to achieve your goals as well.

HENRY FORD—FOUNDER OF FORD MOTOR COMPANY

The man who invented the Model T Ford that revolutionised the automobile industry displayed his characteristic abilities right from a young age. Growing up, his family could not afford farmhands, so he had to help out. In those years, he led his friends in many constructive pursuits and developed his love for machines like steam engines by learning from the men who ran them. There is a story about how Ford got a pocket watch for his 13th birthday, which he promptly took apart. He just wanted to know how it worked, and this was a trait he carried throughout his life—to see how things worked and why they didn't too.

He kept moving from job to job, always learning new things he would use in later life. Ford was a charismatic leader, who dreamed big and had the ability to persuade talented people to join his endeavours. His legacy was the assembly line, which started in the automobile industry and then spread to almost every other manufacturing sector.

KIRAN MAZUMDAR-SHAW—HEAD OF BIOCON

Facing and surmounting incredible obstacles to get where she is, Kiran Mazumdar-Shaw is truly an inspirational personality in the business world today.

With just Rs. 10,000 as capital and a rented garage, she set up the Indian branch of Biocon Biochemicals, Ireland. Gender prejudice, unsupportive banks and her young age (25 years) were against her, but she had the resilience to keep moving and get the funding she needed by knocking on people's doors.

To get skilled people, facilities and equipment for this nascent field of biotechnology was a challenge, but Kiran was never daunted. Thanks to her drive, the company started making profits in the first year itself. Focusing on innovation, research and development, Kiran took the company to greater heights.

She makes the time for philanthropic activities and CSR through her Biocon Foundation that is involved with health, education and infrastructure initiatives in rural areas.

RALPH LAUREN—FOUNDER OF RALPH LAUREN CORPORATION

It was watching his first polo match that inspired him to create the classy, elegant brand Polo Ralph Lauren—now instantly recognised the world over. Born into a poor Jewish immigrant family in the Bronx, Lauren used to escape his poor living conditions by going to the movies. The glamour of that world stayed with him as he ventured into the fashion business.

Always a risk-taker, Lauren started by designing wide, colourful neckties that were the opposite of the prevailing narrow dark ties. These became a runaway hit and set off a new trend. He then started his own company, retailing menswear with a mix of American and British styles and an aura of elegance. Over the years, his brand has branched out into women's and children's clothes, colognes, footwear and other products. What set Lauren apart was his meticulous attention to detail, insistence on superior product quality and the strict control he kept over the brand he had built so carefully over the years.

VANDANA LUTHRA—FOUNDER OF VLCC HEALTHCARE

A global name in beauty and wellness, Vandana had a long road to build the successful empire she heads today. Initially, she met with tremendous resistance to her idea and was ridiculed for the fact that she wanted to become an entrepreneur. Wellness programmes were unheard of at the time and she had an immense task ahead of her to build awareness for her unique concept first. She promoted her company as a clinic and worked hard with doctors, physiotherapists and nutritionists to create the blend of beauty, fitness, nutrition and healthcare that her company is renowned for today. Her customer base keeps growing as they see actual results with her treatments.

VLCC is present across Asia, the Middle East, Africa and Europe, employing over 4,000 people. This Padma Shri awardee is one of the most powerful women in India, and an inspiration for every entrepreneur who has a dream of going global.

WALT DISNEY—FOUNDER OF WALT DISNEY COMPANY

Think of the name Disney and a magical world is conjured up in your mind, populated with the most fascinating characters. He came from a very poor family where they struggled for meals and had to keep moving homes to find suitable work. His father decided to take up farming and it was there that little Walt developed his love for nature and animals that later inspired him to draw Mickey Mouse and Donald Duck.

His first cartoons were bought by the people in his village and soon he started his own studio, which was to become the behemoth Walt Disney Company. Perseverance and sheer talent drove Disney's success in films, amusement parks, merchandise and a variety of spin-offs. His love for the fantasy world earned him a host of awards over the years and won him the love of people of all ages, all around the world.

Integrity for humans is the same. It's not behaviour as much as a combination of things. As we experience life, we learn and develop beliefs and values. When we take action in line with those beliefs and values, we are acting with integrity.

> "Real integrity is doing the right thing, knowing that nobody's going to know whether you did it or not."
> —Oprah Winfrey

The following activities can help one develop strong integrity:

GIVE YOUR WORD AND KEEP IT: By doing this, you display responsibility and commitment, which contribute to building your integrity. However, do not over-commit to a task, just to please or impress someone. You may find that you do not have the time or resources to do it, and when you do not deliver, your reputation suffers. Be honest about your capabilities, as it's okay to say 'No' once in a while.

BE NEAT, LIVE NEATLY: Look in the mirror before you step out—what kind of an impression do you give people? Dressed neatly and being well-groomed shows you care about your personal hygiene and appearance. It's the same attitude that you need to bring to your workspace and home too. Get rid of the clutter, clear out unused and unwanted items and maintain cleanliness. Nowadays, most of your tasks can be done on your mobile phone or computer, eliminating the need for paper. Be organised in your schedule and stick to your appointments as this has a positive impact on people, earning you a reputation for reliability. Set reminders, make lists and keep your family, friends and important contacts informed about your day, so that they can reach you when they need to. It's also important to communicate clearly when speaking or when sending messages, so that people know exactly what you expect of them.

KEEP INSPIRATION AROUND: Surround yourself with things that can influence you positively. Interact with people you enjoy spending time with, who can build you up or who appreciate your company. Spend your commuting time learning more about a topic that interests you, read or listen to something motivational, or simply take in images from the places you're passing by. Volunteer your time to a charitable organisation, as this is where you will meet the most inspiring people. These activities feed your brain in constructive ways and keep you in a positive frame of mind.

STAY AWARE OF YOUR REACTIONS: How you react in any situation shows your character. Join in people's happiness when they share their great or little joys with you and don't try to one-up them or steal the spotlight from them. In challenging times, maintain your cool and think of solutions as people are looking to you for help and do not want blame games.

> "If it is not right, do not do it; if it is not true, do not say it."
>
> —Marcus Aurelius

DEVELOP HABITS THAT ENHANCE YOUR INTEGRITY: You would need to change any negative habits you may have, like finishing people's sentences to hurry them up, procrastinating about making decisions, not giving proper feedback to your team and other detrimental behaviour. Instead, build habits that strengthen your values, and thereby your integrity. For example, cultivate a sympathetic tone and language when speaking with your team about sensitive issues and be assertive when you need to stand up for something.

> "You can fool some of the people all of the time, and all of the people some of the time, but you cannot fool all of the people all of the time."
>
> —Abraham Lincoln

A person of integrity and virtues is truly a trailblazer. Gone are the days when a whiz-kid or adult wizard was given a title based on his awareness of history and geography in the theoretical sense. But when outcomes are based on current information and studying the past, the informed leader becomes a wizard.

In the age of knowledge, the biggest tool is information for making all processes and management efficient. Successful leaders have to be creative and be able to assess and analyse data quickly. They arrive at solutions by thinking out of the box. Aware leaders deal with the situation by thinking on their feet. Leaders take the onus of their decisions and share the fruits of their success with all.

CONCLUSION

People have immense potential to become good leaders. I have been guiding many teachers and students towards success over the years. Certain sections in the book have been taken from my personal experiences which include stories from the lives of a diverse group of people. In each of these anecdotes, the traits that are necessary for being an impactful leader and an asset to society are evident, as every experience in life is enriching.

The book is woven together with the yarn of a strong "I", that is, imagination, insight, intuition, innocence, industriousness, inventiveness, innovativeness, idealism, and intelligence—the many rungs one needs to climb on the ladder to success. Dream big, overcome hurdles by working on yourself and become great leaders.

ABOUT THE AUTHOR

A journey of 34 years in the field of education across schools in India has been enriching and impactful for Kalyani Patnaik. She is a Post-graduate in Economics from Delhi University and completed her Masters in Education from Mumbai University.

She is Principal of Hiranandani Foundation School, HFS International, Powai, in Mumbai and has published articles on education in books and magazines. She is also on the advisory board of non-government organisations working on social causes related to education and upliftment of less-fortunate sections of society.

Fond of writing and motivational speaking, she has conducted in-house workshops for both teachers and parents.

Kalyani Patnaik is settled in Mumbai and has two sons who are based in the USA.